FIFTY
FAVOURITE
NORTHUMBRIAN PUBS

" *The village inn, the dear old inn,*
So ancient, clean and free from sin,
The centre of our rural life
Where Hodge sits down beside his wife
And talks of Manx and nuclear fission
With all the rustic's intuition
Ah, more than church or school or hall
The village inn's the heart of all. "

John Betjeman

ACKNOWLEDGEMENTS

Thanks to all the people involved with the pubs featured in this book for their assistance in ensuring that the information given was up to date at the time of publication. (July 2008).

Photography by the author with additional photographs by Doug Hall, Christopher Moore, Niall Brown, Pat O'Donovan, Phil Huntley and Michael Durnan.

First published in Great Britain in 2008 by *The Northumbrian* magazine (Powdene Publicity Ltd). Unit 17, Quay Level, St. Peter's Wharf, Newcastle upon Tyne, NE6 1TZ.

A catalogue record for this book is available from the British Library

ISBN 978-0-95444-933-9

Printed by Printers Coast Ltd.

FIFTY FAVOURITE NORTHUMBRIAN PUBS

Foreword

AS a by-product of more than 20 years travelling around the county as editor of *The Northumbrian* magazine, the country inns and coastal pubs in this book are either my personal favourites or come highly recommended by the magazine's readers.

Their inclusion may be due to a combination of factors: a perfect location near a tourism hot-spot or off the beaten track, an individual character or old-fashioned style. Some are long established and occupy centuries-old buildings. Others have fascinating collections of local artefacts and memorabilia or a pleasant family-friendly garden. Many serve a wide choice of meals using locally sourced ingredients and almost all of them offer a good choice of cask beers from small, independent Northumbrian brewers.

Among the *Fifty Favourite Pubs* there are places with acclaimed chefs and imaginative à la carte menus where advance booking is essential, while others provide traditional pub meals, open early for breakfast or offer home-made biscuits and cakes.

There are even one or two rare survivals from days past where the only snack is a packet of crisps, and entertainment comes in the form of friendly conversation instead of piped music or the TV screen.

As with many things in life, outward appearances can be deceptive. A pub with an impressive frontage may be a bit of a let-down once you step inside. And pub signs can sometimes be misleading. 'Home-cooked food' sometimes turns out to be ingredients reheated in a microwave oven or boil-in-the-bag pre-prepared meals. 'Food available all day' can translate into 'until the kitchen staff finish work'.

Nor is the day ever likely to come when information displayed outside a pub will warn potential customers that service is neither very speedy nor friendly; that tables in the beer garden are liberally sprinkled with bird droppings; or that while the landlord's wolf-sized dog may be good for deterring burglars, he strongly disapproves of any customer sitting too close to 'his' log fire.

I hope this factual guide will point readers in the right direction – whatever part of Northumberland they happen to be in – with useful information such as opening times, hours when food is available, and whether there is accommodation.

There are frequent references to log fires and sheltered gardens for two simple reasons. In winter months a warm pub is a joy to be in, and while Northumberland does have some warm summer days, there are times when a garden sheltered from chilly winds is a big bonus.

Instead of gushing descriptions and flowery prose, this is a factual guide that will inform the reader whether children are welcome, if the pub is dog-friendly, and even if there is a partially weather-proof outdoor shelter for smokers on a wet and windy night.

This guide will hopefully entice readers to try out a Northumberland pub they have not previously visited, and enjoy a pint of real ale, a meal or an overnight stop whether out for a day's drive or following one of the many long-distance walking or cycling routes in the county.

Information about the pubs in this book was up-to-date at the time of publication and, unlike some pub guides, inclusion in this book did not involve any payment for a mention.

While some country pubs remain in the care of the same families for several generations, changes of ownership do happen, and occasionally a well-run pub can end up in the doldrums very quickly. So in future editions of *Fifty Favourite Pubs* we will take into account reports – good and bad – received from readers along with any recommendations about places not mentioned in this first edition (see page 127).

CONTENTS

Map of pubs: Coast and North 6, 7

Map of pubs: South and West 8, 9

The Coast 11

Coquet Valley 29

Hadrian's Wall 41

North Tyne Valley 51

Mid-Northumberland 61

North Northumberland 73

South West Northumberland 95

Tynedale 107

Local micro-breweries 126

Reader Report 127

Pubs of the Northumberland Coast and in the Coquet Valley, Mid and North-Northumberland.

COAST
1 Crown & Anchor, Holy Island.
2 The Fishing Boat, Boulmer.
3 The Jolly Fisherman, Craster.
4 The Olde Ship, Seahouses.
5 The Red Lion, Alnmouth.
6 The Ship, Holy Island.
7 The Ship, Low Newton-by-the-Sea.
8 Victoria, Bamburgh.

COQUET VALLEY
9 The Angler's Arms, Weldon Bridge.
10 Cross Keys, Thropton.
11 The Rose & Thistle, Alwinton.
12 The Star, Harbottle.
13 The Star, Netherton.

MID-NORTHUMBERLAND
22 The Coach, Lesbury.
23 The Cook & Barker, Newton-on-the-Moor.
24 The Gate, Forestburn Gate.
25 The Horse Shoes, Rennington.
26 The Mason's Arms, Stamford.

NORTH
27 The Anchor, Wooler.
29 The Black Bull, Etal.
30 Black Bull, Lowick.
31 The Blue Bell, Belford.
32 The Percy Arms, Chatton.
33 The Plough, Allerdean.
34 The Red Lion, Milfield.
35 The Tankerville Arms, Eglingham.
36 White Swan, Warenford.

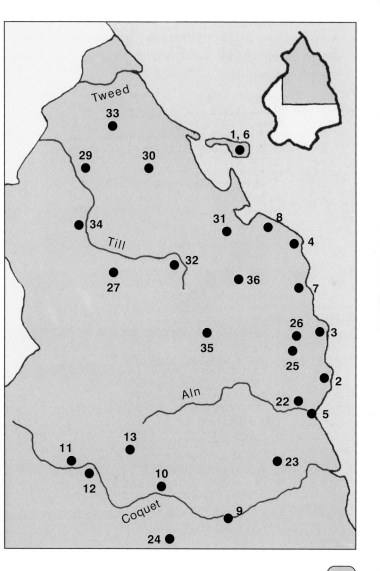

Pubs in the Coquet Valley, Hadrian's Wall country, North Tyne Valley, Mid, North and South West Northumberland and Tynedale.

COQUET VALLEY
9 The Angler's Arms, Weldon Bridge.
10 Cross Keys, Thropton.
11 The Rose & Thistle, Alwinton.
12 The Star, Harbottle.
13 The Star, Netherton.

HADRIAN'S WALL
14 Milecastle, Haltwhistle
15 The Queen's Head, Great Whittington.
16 Robin Hood, East Wallhouses.
17 Twice Brewed, Military Road.

NORTH TYNE VALLEY
18 Battlesteads, Wark.
19 The Black Cock, Falstone.
20 The Pheasant, Stannersburn.
21 Riverdale Hall, Bellingham.

MID-NORTHUMBERLAND
24 The Gate, Forestburn Gate.

NORTH
28 Bay Horse, West Woodburn.

SOUTH-WEST
37 The Allenheads Inn, Allenheads.
38 The Carts Bog, Langley.
39 The Elk's Head, Whitfield.
40 The Golden Lion, Allendale.
41 The Traveller's Rest, Slaley.

TYNEDALE
42 Barrasford Arms, Barrasford.
43 The Black Bull, Corbridge.
44 The Boatside, Warden.
45 Dipton Mill, Dipton Mill.
46 The Feathers, Hedley-on-the-Hill.
47 General Havelock, Haydon Bridge.
48 Lion and Lamb, Horsley.
49 The Rat, Anick.
50 The Railway, Fourstones.

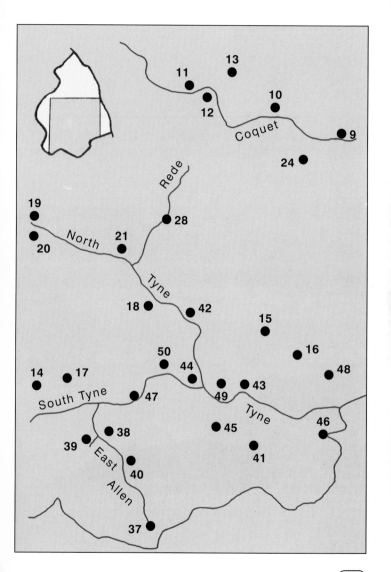

COAST

NORTHUMBERLAND'S beautiful coastline is unique in Britain, with mile upon mile of uncrowded, sandy beaches, a wealth of ancient castles and internationally important wildlife sanctuaries.

By taking a few small diversions off the 64-mile-long Northumberland Coast Path a determined walker could visit all eight of the following pubs in two or three tiring days, but a week would be much more relaxing.

All are found in outstanding locations well worth a visit: on the Holy Island of Lindisfarne; in Bamburgh, the ancient capital of Northumbria; at Seahouses, where boats cross to the Farne Islands; in the traditional fishing villages of Craster, Low Newton-by-the-Sea and Boulmer; and down a cobbled lane in the ancient port of Alnmouth.

Photograph:
Dunstanburgh Castle

(1) *Holy Island* ~
CROWN & ANCHOR INN

THE island is one of the busiest tourist destinations in the county, and from the beer garden of this village centre pub there are close-up views of Lindisfarne Priory and Lindisfarne Castle.

Run by a young couple both born and bred on the island, this 200-year-old inn has an interior with a distinctly individual character. Old photographs of the island's fishing community and paintings by local artists are displayed in the bar and wood-panelled dining room. Tide tables are always available to ensure customers allow enough time for a relaxing drink or meal before the next incoming tide covers the causeway linking Holy Island with the mainland.

Children welcome; dog-friendly.

HOURS OPEN: Easter to October, 11am to 11pm, Mondays to Saturdays; 12 noon to 10pm, Sundays. November to Easter, 11am to 3pm and 6pm to 11pm, Tuesdays to Fridays; 11am to 11pm, Saturdays; Sunday 12 noon to 6pm, Sundays. Between November and February, closed Sunday evenings and Mondays.

BEERS: Guest real ales, Black Sheep, Adnams, Theakstons, John Smith's, Guinness, lagers and Lindisfarne fruit wines.

FOOD: served 12 noon to 2.30pm and 6pm to 8pm, daily (evening bookings advised). Sandwiches and bar meals using locally-sourced meat, fish and vegetables. The lunchtime choice includes soup (£3), sandwiches from £3.50, paninis, jacket potatoes, and local haddock and chips (£7.50).
Specials on the evening menu regularly change. Favourites include a home-made salmon fish cake starter at £3.95, salmon fillet with couscous and asparagus sauce (£11.95), wild mushroom carbonara (£8.95), and, in season, locally-landed lobster and crab.

ACCOMMODATION: three en suite rooms, one room with private bathroom, £80 to £110 per room.

HOW TO GET THERE: turn off the A1 at Beal; travel six miles east to the island causeway, which is cut off for several hours before and after high tide.

**Rachel and Keith Shell,
Crown & Anchor Inn, Market Place,
Holy Island TD15 2RX.
Tel: (01289) 389215.
Email:
crown-anchorinn@holyisland215.wanadoo.co.uk
www.holyislandcrown.co.uk**

(2) *Boulmer* ~
THE FISHING BOAT INN

POPULARLY known as "the FBI", this old pub in the middle of the coast's smallest fishing village has been sensitively modernised and extended by adding a conservatory and deck area overlooking the beach with good views of the fine coastline to the north.

Once famed for its gin smuggling, Boulmer is better known today for having set up its own Volunteer Rescue Service after losing its RNLI lifeboat, and for being the base for the RAF's Sea King Search and Rescue 202 Squadron.

In the bar, lounge and restaurant there is an interesting collection of photographs featuring traditional Northumberland fishing cobles, lifeboats and village fishermen from earlier days and a large

Victorian painting showing the man-and-woman power once needed to launch the village lifeboat.

HOURS OPEN: 12 noon to 3pm and 6.30pm to 11pm, Tuesdays to Sundays; closed Mondays except bank holidays.

BEERS: guest cask ales, plus Tetleys, Guinness and lagers.

FOOD: served 12 noon to 2.15pm daily except Mondays; 6pm to 8pm Tuesdays to Saturdays; Sundays and Mondays in the summer season (advance booking advised).

There is a choice of sandwiches, with chips and salad, at £5.90. A daily blackboard specials menu offers a choice of main courses from £7.90 to £10.90, including steaks, chicken and locally caught seafood including crab, lobster, scampi and wild salmon.

HOW TO GET THERE: follow the minor road from Lesbury, reached via the A1068 from Alnwick; 1½ miles from Longhoughton village.

Michael Boyle,
The Fishing Boat Inn, Boulmer Village,
Alnwick NE66 3BN.
Tel: (01665) 577750.
E-mail: fishingboatinn@aol.com
www.fishingboatinn.co.uk

---

(3) *Craster* ~
THE JOLLY FISHERMAN

PERCHED in a perfect position above the old harbour, this 160-year-old pub has no fancy airs about it, but there is always a friendly atmosphere as locals rub shoulders with a constant flow of visitors seeking refreshment — or shelter — after a coastal walk.

It has a small wood-panelled bar and a larger lounge bar which extends into an upper level room with a picture window overlooking the harbour. There are fine sea views from the beer garden.

Dunstanburgh Castle is only one mile north of the village, and across the road from the pub are Robson's smokehouses where the famous Craster kippers are cured. The pub only has a very small car park, but there are car parks on the road leading into the village.

Children welcome until 9pm; dog-friendly.

HOURS OPEN: summer, 11am to 11pm, daily. Winter, 11am to 3pm and 6pm to 11pm, Mondays to Saturdays; 7pm to 10.30pm, Sundays.

BEERS: Black Sheep, Old Speckled Hen, John Smith's and lagers.

FOOD: served up to 2.30pm in low season, and up to 4pm in summer.

Specialities include crab and salmon sandwiches, home-made Craster kipper pâté and crab-meat soup. Light bites, £2 to £4, include home-made chips, burgers and stottie cake pizza, and there is always a pudding of the day. On Friday nights and occasionally other nights, fish and chips are available at £6.95.

HOW TO GET THERE: follow the B1340 from Alnwick towards Rennington, then take the minor road signposted to Craster.

Billy Silk,
The Jolly Fisherman, Haven Hill, Craster,
Alnwick NE66 3TR.
Tel: (01665) 576461.
Email: Muriel@silk8234.fsnet.co.uk

---

(4) *Seahouses ~*
THE OLDE SHIP HOTEL

STANDING above the busy harbour where visitors embark for tours round the wildlife-rich Farne Islands, this famous pub, run by the same family for 98 years, has an astonishing collection of fishing and seafaring memorabilia.

A gathering place for fishermen since 1812, the 'sea museum' authenticity of the main Saloon Bar includes a wooden floor made from ships' pine decking, sea-themed stained glass windows and an impressive array of artefacts including ships' brass fittings, old seafarers' hats, lobster pots, fishing baskets, diving helmets, oars, figureheads and ships' lamps.

The narrow corridors are filled with photographs recording

generations of Seahouses fishermen. More nautical exhibits are found in the quiet, wood-panelled Cabin Bar, and the Locker Room is awash with model boats, marine charts, ropes and knots.

A garden at the rear of the pub overlooks the harbour and provides a fine view across to the Farne Islands, noted for their seabird and seal colonies.

HOURS OPEN: 11am to 11pm, Mondays to Saturdays; 12 noon to 11pm, Sundays.

BEERS: Ruddles, Black Sheep, Farne Islands Bitter, Courage Directors, Old Speckled Hen, Theakstons, Bass, lagers and a choice of 30 malt whiskies.

FOOD: served 12 noon to 2pm and 7pm to 8.30pm, daily.
Specialities include crab sandwiches, home-made crab soup and Craster kippers. A daily specials board offers a lunchtime choice of six main courses at £7.50. Popular favourites, using locally caught seafood, include bosun's fish stew, smoked fish chowder and fisherman's pie.

ACCOMMODATION: 18 en suite rooms, £56 per person B&B (£48 in low season).

HOW TO GET THERE: from Alnwick follow the B1340 coast road north via Beadnell.

Alan Glen and David Swan,
The Olde Ship Hotel, 9 Main Street,
Seahouses NE68 7RD.
Tel: (01665) 720200.
Email: theoldeship@seahouses.co.uk
www.seahouses.co.uk

---

(5) *Alnmouth ~*
THE RED LION INN

MANY original features have been preserved in this 18th century coaching inn which stands on the village main street and is entered from a cobbled lane where stabling for stagecoach horses was once

provided. Today it is popular with visitors drawn to Alnmouth for the village's fine beach walks.

The lounge bar is full of character, with wood-panelled walls taken from the S.S. Carpathia (the first ship to reach the sinking Titanic), a low beamed ceiling and open fire. The friendly staff provides an efficient, professional service to the steady flow of customers.

The restaurant has been furnished in a light, contemporary style while retaining an old oak-beamed ceiling. At the bottom of the

entrance lane there are a secluded beer garden and an elevated decking area offering fine views over the Aln estuary.
Well-behaved children welcome; dog-friendly.

HOURS OPEN: 9am to 11pm, daily throughout the year.

BEERS: choice of four guest cask ales, Black Sheep, John Smith's, lagers and a choice of 12 wines.

FOOD: served all day from 9am (breakfasts) to 9pm, Mondays to Saturdays; last orders 8pm Sundays.
Sandwiches from £4.25, baguettes from £4.95. Popular starters are Craster kipper pâté, (£5.25) and oak-smoked local salmon with lime, coriander and cucumber salsa (£7.95). Main courses £7.50 to £15.25: house specialities include a large seafood platter with fresh local fish and crab (£11.95), saffron braised lamb shank on roasted red pepper mash, and haddock with home-made chips and mushy peas (£8.95). Children's menu from £3.50.

ACCOMMODATION: five double en suite rooms and one family room; double B&B from £80 to £95.

HOW TO GET THERE: from Alnwick follow the A1068 towards Warkworth. Turn left at roundabout on to the B1339.

Jane and Mac McHugh,
The Red Lion Inn, 22 Northumberland Street,
Alnmouth NE66 2RJ.
Tel: (01665) 830584.
Email: mjmleisureltd@btconnect.com
www.redlionalnmouth.co.uk

(6) *Holy Island* ~
THE SHIP INN

FROM the island's main car parking area, the walking route taken by visitors to reach the National Trust's Lindisfarne Castle and the small island harbour passes this 250 year-old listed building.

The large bar lounge which can seat up to 60 people has a beamed ceiling, wood-panelled walls and, in keeping with the pub's name, a variety of maritime objects ranging from fishermen's knots, a ship's wheel, model boats, a lobster pot and a replica ship's cat — Able Seaman Simon (awarded a posthumous award for bravery).

The seven-table restaurant has exposed stone walls, paintings of sailing ships and a chart recording the many ships wrecked off the nearby Farne Islands. At the rear of the pub a sheltered, well-maintained beer garden which has tables to seat up to 72 people is very popular in summer months.

Children are welcome up to 8pm.

HOURS OPEN: all day in summer. In winter 12 noon to 3pm and 6pm to11pm daily.

BEERS: guest cask beers including Holy Island Blessed Bitter and Theakstons, plus John Smith's, Guinness and lagers.

FOOD: served 12 noon to 2pm and 6pm to 7.30pm, daily.
Sandwiches, bar meals, and an evening à la carte menu. Depending on local catches, fresh fish dishes include mussels cooked in wine (£6.95), whole-tail breaded scampi, plaice and lemon sole goujons, large haddock and chips (£8.50), plus lobster and fresh crab in season. Other popular dishes include home-made beef and Holy Island Ale pie (£10.95).

ACCOMMODATION: four en suite rooms, £72-£112 per room.

HOW TO GET THERE: turn east off the A1 at Beal, then travel six miles to the island causeway, which is closed for several hours before and after high tide.

**Andrew Hnat and Janice Cowan,
The Ship Inn, Marygate, Holy Island TD15 2SJ.
Tel: (01289) 389311.
Email: theshipinn@btconnect.com
www.theshipinn-holyisland.co.uk**

(7) *Low Newton-by-the-Sea ~* **THE SHIP INN**

TUCKED away in a corner of a square enclosed on three sides by old fishermen's cottages, this popular pub which occupies a listed building dating back to 1760 stands just 50 yards from the beach.

Seating for customers inside this small inn can be quickly filled at lunchtimes by walkers following the coastal path between Beadnell and Craster. Tables with a view of the sea on the grassy area in front of the pub help cope with the overflow.

The chance to try cask ales made at the Ship's own micro-brewery is an added attraction. Folk music nights are held on the last Monday of the month. Children are welcome, and so are dogs on leads.

No parking is allowed outside the pub: during the day it costs £2 to use the public car park on the edge of the village; after 6pm it is free.

HOURS OPEN: in summer 11am to11pm, daily; in winter 11am to 3pm daily and 6pm to 11pm Fridays, Saturdays and some Thursdays.

BEERS: cask beers from the pub's own micro-brewery, Dolly Daydream, Ship Hop Ale, Sandcastles at Dawn and Sea Wheat, plus guest beer, John Smith's and lager.

FOOD: served 12 noon to 2.30pm, evenings (booking essential) 7pm to 8pm.

Soup, sandwiches, ploughman's at lunchtime. Favourites on the small evening menu, which changes daily, include fresh crab salad, steaks, venison, a vegetarian choice and freshly caught fish. Between June and October lobster caught in Newton Bay can be pre-ordered at £22. Old fashioned, home-made puddings are a speciality. No credit or debit cards accepted.

HOW TO GET THERE: from the A1 north of Alnwick, take the B6347 via Christon Bank; cross the B1340 and go through High Newton-by-the-Sea on to Low Newton. Car park on hill before entering village.

**Christine Forsyth,
The Ship Inn, Newton-by-the-Sea,
Alnwick NE66 3EL.
Tel: (01665) 576262.
www.shipinnnewton.co.uk**

---

(8) *Bamburgh ~*
VICTORIA HOTEL

THIS historic village became the centre of worldwide attention in 1838 thanks to the heroic exploits of 22-year-old lighthouse keeper's daughter Grace Darling, who risked her life to rescue

shipwreck survivors in raging seas off the Farne Islands. The RNLI Grace Darling Museum and Bamburgh Castle are both within a few minutes' walk.

Originally built in 1876 as two private houses overlooking the attractive village green, the Victoria opened as a hotel in 1926, and in complete contrast to its slightly austere outward appearance, the lounge bar has a smart, modern Scandinavian feel with light, wood-panelled walls and floors. The spacious lounge bar has a more decorative style, with chandeliers and a multitude of wall mirrors. The Brasserie restaurant has 20 tables in a glass-domed conservatory and an adjoining dining area.

HOURS OPEN: 11am to 11pm, daily.

BEERS: Black Sheep, John Smith's, Guinness, lagers, cider and a choice of 28 wines.

FOOD: teas, coffees and bar meals served from 12 noon to 8.30pm.
The Brasserie, with à la carte menu, is open for Sunday lunches and in the evenings from 6.30pm (advance booking is advised).
Sandwiches £4.25. Bar menu starters from £3.75. Popular main courses, from £7.50, include lamb shank, Bamburgh bangers from next-door butchers Robert Carter & Son, and haddock in beer batter.
Children's menu £3.95.

ACCOMMODATION: 37 en suite rooms, from £50 per person B&B.

HOW TO GET THERE: follow the B1341 to the coast from the A1 at Adderstone.

Graham Young,
Victoria Hotel, 1 Front Street,
Bamburgh NE69 7BP.
Tel: (01668) 214431.
Email: enquiries@thevictoriahotelbamburgh.co.uk

COQUET VALLEY

RISING high in the Cheviot Hills, the River Coquet travels through the wild hill country and picturesque valleys within Northumberland National Park, then flows past villages and farmland on its seaward journey.

Pubs featured in this section are found in the quiet upper Coquetdale villages of Alwinton, Harbottle, Netherton and Thropton; and at Weldon Bridge — a short drive from Brinkburn Priory and the National Trust-owned palatial house and extensive wooded grounds of Cragside, created by Victorian armaments magnate, Lord Armstrong.

Information about the valley's wide choice of walks and footpaths is available from the national park visitor centre in Rothbury.

Photograph:
Harbottle Crags

(9) *Weldon Bridge* ~
THE ANGLER'S ARMS

THIS traditional coaching inn which dates back to the 1760s is a large busy pub in a picturesque setting on the north bank of the River Coquet next to the old stone-built Weldon Bridge. Aptly, given the

pub's name, the oak-panelled bar and lounge contain an interesting display of fishing rods, salmon flies and other angling memorabilia.

The pub has a busy lunchtime and evening meal trade and, in addition to tables in the comfortable, wood-panelled lounge where brass pans and jugs are suspended from ceiling beams, food is also served in an adjoining dining room decorated with angling prints and in a Pullman railway carriage linked to the main building.

The beer garden has outdoor tables and a children's play area.

HOURS OPEN: 11am to 11pm, Mondays to Saturdays; 12 noon to 10.30pm, Sundays.

BEERS: a choice of four guest cask beers, usually including Timothy Taylor Landlord, Black Sheep, Old Speckled Hen and Theakstons, plus Worthington, Guinness and lagers. Wines by the glass £3.50.

FOOD: served 12 noon to 9.30pm, Mondays to Saturdays; 12 noon to 9pm, Sundays.

Sandwiches, bar meals and an à la carte restaurant. Bar menu and daily specials board main courses from £8.45, including farmhouse mixed grill and Northumbrian sausage casserole. Restaurant menu main courses from £14.95 to £19.50 including Border rack of lamb and cod and crab fishcakes. Vegetarian dishes £9.75. Children's menu £4.95.

ACCOMMODATION: seven en suite rooms. B&B double £75, single £42.50, family room £100 for four guests (£90 for two).

HOW TO GET THERE: turn off the A697 Coldstream road for Rothbury nine miles north of Morpeth; Weldon Bridge is 5¹/2 miles east of the National Trust's Cragside Estate.

**John and Julie Young,
The Angler's Arms, Weldon Bridge,
Longframlington NE65 8AX.
Tel: (01665) 570271.
Email: johnyoung@anglersarms.fsnet.co.uk
www.anglersarms.com**

---

(10) *Thropton ~*
CROSS KEYS

A PHOTOGRAPH on display in this compact, stone-built village pub
shows it has been open for business since at least 1832. It
traditional bar with half wood-panelled walls is a meeting place fo

locals and popular with visitors heading further west into Uppe
Coquetdale, the Cheviot Hills and Northumberland National Park.

There are tables for diners in a small snug, and the seven-tabl
restaurant — which displays pen-and-ink drawings of local scenes —
looks out onto a sloping beer garden. This has a series of terrace
and from its upper level there is a fine view extending west into th
Cheviot Hills.

The Cross Keys is dog-friendly and children are welcome.

HOURS OPEN: 11am to 11pm, daily.

BEERS: Old Speckled Hen, Black Sheep, John Smith's, Bass, Worthington, Guinness, lagers and a choice of 14 wines.

FOOD: served 12 noon to 3pm and 6 to 9pm, daily.
Sandwiches, bar meals and a restaurant menu: main courses from £6.95 to £13.50. There is a daily fish menu (£4.95 to £11.95) usually offering a choice of lemon sole, sea bass, cod, haddock, rainbow trout, bream and scampi. In addition to dishes using locally-sourced meat, the menu also offers a choice of five vegetarian meals and a range of salads. A three-course Sunday lunch is £9.95.

HOW TO GET THERE: Thropton is two miles west of Rothbury along the B6341.

Gail Hooper and George Yule,
Cross Keys, Thropton, Rothbury NE65 7HX.
Tel: (01669) 620362.
Email: gailcrosskeys@yahoo.co.uk

---

(11) *Alwinton* ~
THE ROSE & THISTLE INN

PARTS of this outwardly unassuming single-storey stone building date back to the 13th century, and it was probably an alehouse serving this remote part of Upper Coquetdale long before it became a coaching inn during the mid-18th century.

Run by the same family for 100 years, this Tardis-like pub is much larger than its outward appearance suggests. The traditional, stone-floored bar is filled with old photographs and drawings, fishing and hunting memorabilia and collections of rifle and artillery shells which, alongside a collection of regimental cap badges, underline the closeness of the Otterburn military ranges.

Standing at the edge of the Cheviot foothills, Alwinton is a favourite with hill walkers and the pub provides a drying room for boots and outdoor clothing – a useful facility that was not available when Sir Walter Scott stayed here while writing 'Rob Roy'. There is also a storage garage for bikes.

Behind the old bar there is a large lounge which overlooks an attractive beer garden offering a fine view across the valley.

HOURS OPEN: 12 noon to 3pm and 7pm to 11pm, Tuesdays to Fridays; 12 noon to 5pm and 7pm to 11pm Saturdays and Sundays; 7pm to 11pm Mondays.

BEERS: Farne Islands Bitter, Tetleys, Boddingtons, Guinness and lagers.

FOOD: served 12 noon to 2.30pm and 7pm to 9pm, Tuesdays to Saturdays; 12 noon to 2.30pm Sundays.
Sandwiches and bar meals £3-£10.95; three-course Sunday lunch £9.95. Popular dishes include steak pie, and home-cooked ham with salad.

ACCOMMODATION: three en suite bedrooms, B&B £29 per person, single £35.

HOW TO GET THERE: travel west from Rothbury on the B6341 to Flotterton, then follow the road signposted to Sharperton, Harbottle and Alwinton.

Gareth and Jane Latcham,
The Rose & Thistle Inn, Alwinton,
Rothbury, NE65 7BQ.
Tel: (01669) 650226.
Email: enqs@roseandthistlealwinton.com
www.roseandthistlealwinton.com

---

(12) *Harbottle ~*
THE STAR INN

BUILT from locally quarried stone as a 'model' pub in the early 1800s, the Star has been run by the same husband-and-wife team for more than 30 years, and villagers are proud of its genuine old-fashioned atmosphere.

The traditional bar, which has old fixed seating and matchboard wall panelling, has coal and log fires in winter months when it is frequently used by various village groups for their meetings. It also hosts the local leek, onion and potato shows and presents occasional music nights.

There is a small pool room which, in summer months, is turned into the village craft centre, and the pub's original 'snug' now serves as both the village newsagents and a Northumberland National Park information point. The Star is unable to provide food or accommodation, nor is there room for children or dogs in its single public room, but it is worth a visit.

The remains of Harbottle Castle, built by Henry II in the late 12th century and once owned by the powerful Umfraville family, lie on the western edge of the village and the site is open to the public.

HOURS OPEN: 12noon to 3pm and 6pm to 11pm, daily.

BEERS: John Smith's, McEwan's Best Scotch, lager.

HOW TO GET THERE: travel west from Rothbury on the B6341 to Flotterton, then turn right on the road signposted to Sharperton, Harbottle and Alwinton.

**Robert and Anne Dunn,
The Star Inn, Harbottle, Morpeth, NE65 7DG.
Tel: (01669) 650221.**

(13) Netherton ~
THE STAR INN

THIS unique pub, which dates back to 1788, has been privately owned by the same family since 1917. The long-serving landlady, who was born on the premises, can categorically confirm that it has remained unchanged for 80 years.

The only pub in the county to have appeared in every edition of the CAMRA Good Beer Guide, it has one high-ceilinged room with wooden benches and a 1950s tiled fireplace. Cask beer from the cellar is served from a hatch in the hallway.

This classic pub from a bygone age has outside toilets and, unsurprisingly, it does not serve food. Dogs and children are not admitted but there are a few outside tables.

Regulars from the village and nearby hill farms are used to its limited opening hours, while first-time visitors are often disappointed to find it closed at lunchtimes and all day on Mondays and Thursdays. Quiz nights are held on the first Wednesday of each month from March to November.

HOURS OPEN: 7.30pm to 10pm, Tuesdays and Wednesdays; 7.30pm to 11pm, Fridays; 7.30pm to 10.30pm, Saturdays and Sundays. Closed Mondays and Thursdays.

BEER: Castle Eden Ales.

HOW TO GET THERE: follow the B6341 from Rothbury to Thropton. Turn right at the Cross Keys, then turn right on the road through Snitter to Netherton.

Vera W. Wilson-Morton,
The Star Inn, Netherton, Thropton NE65 7HD.
Tel: (01669) 630238.

HADRIAN'S WALL

BUILT on the orders of the Emperor Hadrian in the 2nd century AD, the 73-mile-long Roman Wall formed a defensive barrier 12 feet high which stretched from the Tyne to the Solway Firth.

Acknowledged to be the best preserved frontier of the Roman Empire, the Wall has World Heritage Site status, and the excavated forts at Housesteads, Chesters and Vindolanda attract large numbers of overseas visitors.

The 81-mile-long Hadrian's Wall Path, which runs from Wallsend to Bowness-on-Solway, has quickly become one of the most popular national walking trails in the country.

Three of the pubs in this section stand on the Military Road, built alongside the Wall in the18th century. The fourth is found in the village of Great Whittington, just to the north of the Wall, which lies on the 97-mile-long St Oswald's Way trail from Holy Island to Heavenfield, near Chollerford.

Photograph:
Crag Lough

(14) *Haltwhistle ~* **Milecastle Inn**

ESTABLISHED as an inn back in the 1830s in a building that dates back to the 1700s, the pub's position on the Military Road near one of the best sections of Hadrian's Wall makes it a magnet for summer tourists. Children are welcome.

It has an attractive traditional bar with wood settles, low beamed ceiling, wood panelling, lots of prints and an open fire. Windows in the bar and dining room overlook the Roman Wall, which can also be viewed from a small beer garden.

The Milecastle is a popular rest stop for cyclists travelling the Hadrian's Wall cycle route, and walkers following the long distance Hadrian's Wall Path or the Pennine Way. It is believed that past celebrity visitors including Mick Jagger and Spike Milligan probably arrived by car.

HOURS OPEN: 12 noon to 11pm, daily in spring and summer; 12 noon to 3pm and 6pm to10pm in winter.

BEERS: cask ales Castle Eden, Prince Bishop (from the Big Lamp Brewery), Tetleys, Guinness, lagers and a choice of 10 malt whiskies.

FOOD: served 12 noon to 9pm, spring and summer; 12 noon to 3pm and 6pm to 9pm from October into winter.

Extensive blackboard bar meal choice, restaurant menu and children's menu. A wide choice of food includes nine starters, 16 main courses including honey roast half duck, beef and venison poacher's pie, pheasant in garlic and Madeira, and venison casserole. Main courses £7.95 to £14.95.

ACCOMMODATION: two holiday cottages to let (three nights minimum stay).

HOW TO GET THERE: from Housesteads Roman Fort, travel west along the B6318 (Military Road) for five miles.

**Kevin and Clare Hind,
Milecastle Inn, North Road,
Haltwhistle NE49 9NN.
Tel: (01434) 321372.
Email: clarehind@aol.com
www.milecastle-inn.co.uk**

---

(15) *Great Whittington ~*
THE QUEEN'S HEAD INN

NORTHUMBERLAND'S oldest coaching inn, built in 1615, this recently refurbished village pub has a highly experienced chef and a well established reputation for good food.

Popular with visitors heading towards the central section of Hadrian's Wall, a few miles further west, and a convenient refreshment halt for walkers following the St. Oswald's Way long distance footpath, it has a standing bar that features a large hunting mural above an old fireplace with log fire. Food is served in a comfortable lounge displaying paintings by local artists and a pleasant 10 table restaurant plus a snug dining area seating 12. Situated on the edge of this quiet village, the pub's beer garden overlooks open countryside.

HOURS OPEN: 12 noon to 3pm, and 5.30pm to 11pm, Monday to Thursday.
12noon to midnight, Friday and Saturday. 12 noon to 10.30pm, Sunday.

BEERS: A changing selection of locally brewed guest beers including Fifth Anniversary and Nel's Best from nearby High House Farm Brewery, John Smiths, McEwans Scotch, Guinness and lagers. Choice of 11 wines.

FOOD: served 12 noon to 2.30pm, 6-9pm, Monday to Thursday. 12 noon to 9.30pm, Friday and Saturday. 12 noon to 6pm, Sunday. (Advance booking advised).
A speciality is beef and lamb reared on the neighbouring East Farm. Light bites from £4.95, hot-filled beef, lamb or pork stotties, £5.95. The frequently changing day menu, served to 7pm, has starters from £3.95. Mains from £7.95 to £12.50, include Seared Great Whittington lambs liver, bacon and black pudding.
Dinner menu favourites include a Confit duck leg pancake, pan roasted rump of Galloway beef from East Farm, £12.50, homemade fish and prawn pie, £9.50.

HOW TO GET THERE: From the A68 roundabout at Stagshaw, travel east along the B6318 (Military Road), then turn left and follow a minor road for 1 1/2 miles to the village.

Claire and Steven Murray
The Queen's Head Inn,
Great Whittington, NE19 2HP.
Tel: 01434-672267.
Email: clairemurray3@btinternet.com

---

(16) *East Wallhouses ~*
ROBIN HOOD INN

THIS traditional country pub stands on the old Military Road on the vallum side of Hadrian's Wall, and the men who built it in 1752 very probably 'borrowed' stones originally used by the Romans.

Lying alongside the Hadrian's Wall Path, it's a popular rest stop for thirsty walkers and an official stamping station for those attempting the full coast-to-coast marathon trek. The Hadrian's Wall Country bus service AD122, which operates in the summer months, also stops here.

Inside, an old-fashioned atmosphere has been deliberately retained with beamed ceilings and open log fires in winter months. The wood-panelled lounge bar has oak settles with characters from the turf and hunting worlds hand-carved into arm rests.

The 60-seat restaurant, which has a distinctive rustic décor, a large old stone fireplace and an interesting clutter of antiques and curios, overlooks a rear patio area and beer garden with views over open farmland to the north.

HOURS OPEN: 11am to 11pm, Mondays to Saturdays; 11am to 10.30pm, Sundays.

BEERS: a changing selection of three or four cask ales, usually including the local Wylam Gold Tankard; plus John Smith's, McEwan's, Guinness, lagers and a choice of 22 wines.

FOOD: served 12 noon to 9.30pm, daily (advance booking advised for Sunday lunch).

Sandwiches (£5.95), a daily specials board, vegetarian meals and à la carte menu all feature Northumbrian meat and other locally-sourced produce. Starters from £3.95; main courses from £9.95, favourites among which include beef and leek dumplings, a choice of five steaks, rack of lamb, and a selection of fish dishes. Special nights feature fish on Wednesdays, steak on Thursdays, and there are occasional tapas and curry nights.

HOW TO GET THERE: travel east for 3 1/2 miles along the B6318 Military Road from the Stagshaw roundabout junction of the A68.

Susan Wilson,
Robin Hood Inn, East Wallhouses NE18 0LL.
Tel: (01434) 672273.
Email: enquiries@robinhoodnorthumberland.co.uk
www.robinhoodnorthumberland.co.uk

(17) *Military Road ~* ***Twice Brewed Inn***

THIS large, recently refurbished roadside inn has been here since the 1800s. Windows in the large bar area offer views of Hadrian's Wall and there is also a comfortable lounge area and a restaurant with

south-facing views. The sheltered beer garden is also south facing.

The legend that the inn's name was inspired by the men building the Military Road in the 18th century who complained that the area's weak beer needed brewing again is, apparently, untrue. Earlier, older inns in the vicinity were known as East Twice Brewed and West Twice Brewed and served travellers using an old drovers' road that passed between two hills known as 'brews'.

Children are welcome. Internet access is available and the pub is close to both the Northumberland National Park visitor centre and Once Brewed Youth Hostel.

HOURS OPEN: 11am to 11pm, Mondays to Saturdays in summer (12 noon to 11pm in winter); 12 noon to 10.30pm, Sundays.

BEERS: Twice Brewed Bitter, Red Shep, plus other guest cask ales from High House and Allendale breweries, Boddingtons, Guinness, lagers and a choice of 25 wines.

FOOD: served 12 noon to 6pm, Mondays to Saturdays; 6pm to 8pm, Mondays to Thursdays; 6pm to 8.30pm Fridays and Saturdays; Sunday lunches from 12 noon.

The bar menu offers baguettes and main courses from £6.25 including Northumbrian beef and Guinness cobbler, home-made steak pie and Northumbrian farmhouse sausages. The evening menu offers starters from £3.95. Main course house favourites, from £7.75, include salad, breaded whole-tail scampi, gammon, steaks and a choice of four vegetarian dishes.

ACCOMMODATION: 14 rooms, £28 to £70 B&B.

HOW TO GET THERE: from Housesteads Roman Fort, travel west along the B6318 (Military Road) for $2^{1}/2$ miles.

Brian Keen,
Twice Brewed Inn, Military Road,
Bardon Mill NE47 7AN.
Tel: (01434) 344534.
Email: info@twicebrewedinn.co.uk

NORTH TYNE VALLEY

RISING on the border between England and Scotland on Peel Fell, the North Tyne was dammed in 1980 to form Kielder Water, one of the largest man-made lakes in north-west Europe.

The seven-mile-long reservoir is encircled by the 125,000-acre Kielder Forest, and the road running up the valley to Kielder village has fine lakeside views, car parks and picnic areas. Visitor centres are located at Tower Knowe and Kielder Castle.

There is a wide range of way-marked walking trails, lakeside walks and off-road cycle routes, and the lake is popular with anglers, sailors, windsurfers and water skiers.

Pubs in this section are located at Falstone and Stannersburn close to the Kielder Dam; lower down the valley in the ancient market town of Bellingham; and in Wark, the 'capital' of Tynedale in the 13th century when the area was under Scottish rule.

Photograph:
Kielder Water and Forest

(18) *Wark ~*
BATTLESTEADS HOTEL

ON the southern edge of this historic North Tyne village, the family-run Battlesteads occupies a mid-18th century farmhouse which has been considerably extended and recently refurbished to a high standard.

The smart, spacious bar has a beamed ceiling, and a comfortable lounge area is furnished with leather armchairs and has a wood-burning stove. There is an 80-seat restaurant, a large conservatory overlooking a secluded, walled garden and a terrace with outdoor tables. Children and dogs are welcome in the bar.

Wark is close to the Pennine Way and the area offers a wide choice of riverside and country walks.

HOURS OPEN: 11am to 11pm, daily.

_____

BEERS: Durham Magus, Black Sheep Bitter and three guest real ales. There's a choice of 20 wines and this former temperance hotel still offers ginger beer, organic lemonade and dandelion and burdock.

_____

FOOD: served from 12 noon to 3pm and 6.30pm to 9.30pm, daily. Snacks, bar meals and á la carte menu. Set lunch, two courses £10.50; set dinner, two courses £17.50. This is sheep country, so lamb steaks and cutlets are a speciality along with other fresh, seasonal local produce. Other popular dishes include a Northumbrian platter of locally smoked meats, fish and cheese.

_____

ACCOMMODATION: 17 en suite rooms (four ground floor rooms with disabled access), £45-£50 per person B&B.

_____

HOW TO GET THERE: Wark is on the B6320, three miles south of Bellingham.

_____

Richard Slade,
Battlesteads Hotel, Wark, Hexham, NE48 3LS.
Tel: (01434) 230209.
Email: info@battlesteads.com
www.battlesteads-hotel.co.uk

_____

(19) *Falstone ~*
THE BLACKCOCK INN

LOCATED on the western edge of Northumberland National Park, Falstone is close to a network of way-marked walks and off-road cycle trails in and around Kielder Water and Kielder Forest.

This stone-built 17th century village inn close to Kielder Water has a comfortable bar, warmed in winter by a wood-burning black-leaded range. It is filled with interesting local information such as illustrated maps which show places to fish and play golf, plus guides to museums, castles, nature trails and forest walks. In addition to the bar, food is also served in Chatto's restaurant and on one side of the pub, next to St Peter's Church, there is a small, sheltered beer garden.

Apart from its popularity with visitors and water sports

enthusiasts attracted to Britain's largest man-made reservoir, pub regulars include villagers, forestry workers and farmers. It has a thriving leek club and offers a take-away meals service.

Children welcome; dog-friendly.

HOURS OPEN: 12 noon to 2pm, Wednesdays to Fridays; 12 noon to 3pm, Saturdays and Sundays; 7pm to 11pm, Mondays to Saturdays; 7pm to 10.30pm, Sundays. Closed Tuesdays.

BEERS: guest cask beer changes weekly, plus John Smith's, Worthington, Guinness and lagers. A selection of 30 malt whiskies and 17 wines.

FOOD: served 12 noon to 2pm, Wednesdays to Sundays; 7pm to 8.30pm, Wednesdays to Mondays.

Lunch menu, £3.45 to £9.95, offers light meals and traditional favourites such as toad in the hole. An à la carte evening menu, main courses £9.95 to £13.95, features Northumbrian steaks, lamb shank, and a Catch of the Day special often featuring exotic fish. Children's menu and a good choice of vegetarian meals.

ACCOMMODATION: six en suite rooms, double B&B £70 per person, family room from £105 for three people.

HOW TO GET THERE: follow the Kielder Water road from Bellingham for 81/2 miles and turn right just beyond Stannersburn into Falstone village.

**Derek and Tracy,
The Blackcock Inn, Falstone,
Kielder Water NE48 1AA.
Tel: (01434) 240200.
Email: thebcinn@yahoo.co.uk
www.blackcockinn.co.uk**

---

(20) *Stannersburn* ~ **THE PHEASANT INN**

ONCE a rough and ready 18th century ale house, the Pheasant is now a successful, family-run business with an established reputation for good, traditional English food. Its two comfortable, well-

furnished bars contain an interesting collection of old photographs depicting life in the valley before it was flooded early in the1980s to create Kielder Water.

There is also a quiet, wood-panelled lounge and an attractive restaurant with views over the North Tyne valley. Outdoor tables are provided in the front forecourt and in the garden, which has a stream running through it. Children are welcome but no dogs are allowed in the main building.

The Pheasant is a popular base for anglers, walkers, cyclists and water sports enthusiasts who sail and water-ski a few miles up the road on Britain's largest man-made lake.

HOURS OPEN: April to October, 11am to 3pm and 6.30pm to 11pm, Mondays to Saturdays, 12 noon to 3pm and 7pm to 11pm, Sundays. November to March, 12 noon to 2.30pm and 7pm to11pm, Wednesdays to Sundays; closed Mondays and Tuesdays.

BEERS: Timothy Taylor's Landlord and a selection of cask beers from Wylam Brewery, plus John Smith's and a good selection of wines and malt whiskies.

FOOD: served 12 noon to 2.30pm and 7pm to 9pm, daily.
Sandwiches, bar meals and a restaurant menu. Chef and co-proprietor, Robin Kershaw, uses locally-sourced meat, fish and vegetables. Specialities include slow-roasted Northumberland lamb, baked gammon with a Cumberland sauce, and home-made game and mushroom pie. Bar lunches from £7.50 to £9.50; evening main dishes from £7.95 to £16.50.

ACCOMMODATION: eight en suite rooms in converted barns and cottages overlooking a garden courtyard. B&B single rooms from £50, doubles from £80.

HOW TO GET THERE: from Bellingham follow the Kielder Water road west for eight miles.

**Walter and Robin Kershaw,
The Pheasant Inn, Stannersburn,
Kielder Water NE48 1DD.
Tel: (01434) 240382.
Email: enquiries@thepheasantinn.com**

(21) *Bellingham ~*
RIVERDALE HALL HOTEL

THERE'S a relaxed, informal atmosphere in this Victorian country house largely created by owner, John Cocker, who has run Riverdale with his family for 30 years.

The bar is filled with cricket, angling and golf memorabilia collected by the sports-mad landlord, who played water polo for England and professional football for Halifax Town. The bar and two lounges look out onto a sun terrace and Riverdale's own cricket field where the veteran 'home' team, Cocker's Knockers, play visiting teams.

Voted the best hotel in England and Wales for salmon fishing, Riverdale has its own 'beats' on the North Tyne which produce mpressive hauls of salmon, sea trout and wild brown trout between May and October. At only £50 a day, Riverdale's salmon fishing is a bargain. Bellingham golf course is across the road and non-resident liners can use the hotel's indoor swimming pool.

Children welcome; dog-friendly except in the restaurant.

HOURS OPEN: all day, every day until "the last customer's bedtime".

BEERS: guest real ales, Tetleys, Guinness, cider and lagers, plus a choice of 100 wines.

FOOD: served 12 noon to 2.30pm and 6pm to 9.30pm, daily.
Sandwiches, bar meals and à la carte menu. Riverdale has a large team of chefs and up to 100 people can be seated in the dining room and adjoining conservatory of this Les Routiers Gold Plate award-winning restaurant. Lunch menus (from £8.90 for one course) and dinner menus (from £18.90 for two courses) change every day. Popular dishes include venison Wellington, pheasant and rabbit pie, and North Tyne salmon and sea trout.

ACCOMMODATION: 33 en suite rooms, B&B double from £58 per person, single £69, plus four self-catering apartments.

HOW TO GET THERE: Riverdale Hall stands on the western edge of Bellingham, on the road to Kielder Water.

John Cocker,
Riverdale Hall Hotel, Bellingham NE48 2JT.
Tel: (01434) 220254.
Email: reservations@riverdalehallhotel.co.uk

MID-NORTHUMBERLAND

AWAY from the busy tourist destinations, this central area of the county has numerous attractive, unspoilt villages with traditional pubs that serve as a focal point for the local communities as well as offering a welcome to visitors.

In the countryside around them there is a thriving farming scene comprising arable crops, beef cattle and sheep, and these favourite pubs pride themselves on offering locally-sourced food.

Most of the pubs in this section are within a short drive of Alnwick, where the castle — the ancestral seat of the Dukes of Northumberland — and the new Alnwick Garden are the principal attractions.

The villages of Lesbury and Rennington lie to the east of the A1; Newton-on-the-Moor lies just off the A1 to the south of Alnwick; and to the south west, Forestburn Gate stands in a secluded valley near the Simonside Hills.

Photograph:
Alnwick Castle

(22) *Lesbury ~*
THE COACH INN

THIS attractive stone-built pub in the village's main street is noted for its colourful displays of flower-filled baskets and tubs and attractive, thatch-topped outdoor tables.

An inn that dates back to the 1750s and originally called the Blacksmith's Arms, it was forced to close in 1896 following a complaint about noisy customers — navvies building the nearby section of the London to Edinburgh railway line — made by the Dowager Duchess of Northumberland who then lived in a grand house across the road. It was reopened as a pub in 1986 by the owner of the Alnwick Rum Company.

The attractive lounge bar has a low beamed ceiling, there is a quiet snug with leather settees and armchairs, and the dining room occupies what was once the village blacksmith's shop. At the rear of the pub there is a car park and a sheltered beer garden.

Children are allowed in the dining room up to 7.30pm.

HOURS OPEN: 11am to 11pm, daily.

BEERS: Black Sheep, McEwan's Best Scotch, Stones, Worthington and lagers. There is a good range of wines.

FOOD: served from 12 noon until 8.30-9pm daily. In winter months 12 noon to 5pm on Sundays.

Sandwiches from £4.20 and light bites, together with full menu served all day. Starters, from £4.20, include local Lindisfarne mussels and grilled Craster kipper. Popular house specials, from £7.20, include fresh cod landed from Amble, local crab, braised Northumbrian beef with leek pudding (£9.60) and slow-roasted local lamb. Also a good vegetarian choice and children's menu. Puddings all £4.20.

HOW TO GET THERE: from Alnwick, travel east along the A1068.

Susan Packard,
The Coach Inn, Lesbury, Alnwick NE66 3PP.
Tel: (01665) 830265.
Email: susanpackard@btconnect.com

---

(23) *Newton-on-the-Moor ~*
THE COOK AND BARKER INN

NAMED after local 19th century landowner, Samuel Cook, who married one Elizabeth Barker, this attractive old coaching inn stands on the edge of a hillside village just off the A1 south of Alnwick.

The smartly furnished pub is a long-established family business and has a busy bar with a log fire in an old range and a brass railed bar counter. Meals are served here and in two restaurant areas, the larger of which has a farmhouse feel with exposed beams and a mix of wood-panelled and stone walls, while the other is a more intimate room with a snug and a small private dining room. There is a small sheltered beer garden and outdoor tables in front of the pub with views across to the coast.

Children welcome.

HOURS OPEN: 11am to 11pm, daily.

BEERS: a choice of guest cask beers usually including Black Sheep, Landlord, London Pride, Secret Kingdom, and Theakstons, plus Caffreys, Worthington, Guinness, lagers and an extensive wine list.

FOOD: served 12 noon to 2pm and 6pm to 9pm, Mondays to Saturdays, and all day from 12 noon on Sundays. Advance booking advised.

Sandwiches and baguettes are served all day. The bar meal menu changes daily. Evening restaurant service offers à la carte and table d'hôte menus, in which the emphasis is on locally-sourced produce including pork from the family farm, locally-reared organic lamb and beef, fish and vegetables. A daily specials board offers starters from £4.25, a choice of six vegetarian meals, and popular main courses include steak and onion pie at £7.95 and slow-roasted belly pork with seared scallops and a red pepper pesto, £12.50.

ACCOMMODATION: 19 double and twin en suite rooms; single B&B £57, double £75.

HOW TO GET THERE: take the Newton-on-the-Moor exit off the A1 five miles south of Alnwick.

Phil Farmer,
The Cook & Barker Inn, Newton-on-the-Moor,
Felton, Morpeth NE65 9JY.
Tel: (01665) 575234.
www.cookandbarkerinn.co.uk

---

(24) *Forestburn Gate ~* THE GATE

STANDING in a wooded valley near the Simonside Hills, this really old-fashioned country pub was built in about 1826. Daytime visitors are invited to walk in and ring the bell on the counter to give the landlady a 'customer alert'.

In the small no-frills bar which overlooks the tree-fringed Forest Burn, there are bench seats, floral wallpaper, an open fire, a darts board and a collection of old photographs of local people and places.

There is also a small snug and a music room which features traditional accordion music on the last Wednesday of every month. Poetry nights are held here on the second Tuesday of every month with The Gate's resident poet, Peter Athey.

The village that once stood here is now gone, but the pub remains an evening gathering point for the nearby rural community and farms. Visitors are given a warm welcome, as are children, until 9pm. Dog friendly. There are a few tables in the courtyard and a shelter for smokers near the outside men's toilet.

The pub hosts two special fundraising events every year: the Hay Show in February and the Simonside Country Fair in August. It is close to the Simonside Forest Trails, and day fishing is available at nearby Fontburn Reservoir.

HOURS OPEN: 11am to 11pm, Mondays to Saturdays; 12 noon to 10.30pm, Sundays.

BEERS: Tetleys, Theakstons, Northumbrian Smooth, Guinness and lager; Strongbow cider.

FOOD: only soup and sandwiches, made on request. Home-pickled eggs from the landlady's free-range chickens.

HOW TO GET THERE: on the B6342, four miles south of Rothbury.

Val Brown,
The Gate, Forestburn Gate, Netherwitton,
Morpeth NE61 4PT.
Tel: (01669) 620643.
Email: Valerie_Brown@btconnect.com

(25) *Rennington* ~
THE HORSE SHOES INN

THE social hub of this quiet village, this traditional, family-run pub which has been in business since 1851 is part of an attractive row of stone cottages built in 1720 with an upper floor added a century later. In the bar, with a large stone fireplace, beamed ceiling and

dried hops hanging above the serving counter, visitors placing food orders often mingle with domino-playing locals before moving through into a two-room, 50-seat restaurant that fills the space once occupied by the village blacksmith.

The attractive beer garden is a peaceful spot unless you happen to be there on August Bank Holiday Saturday. That's the day of the annual scarecrow competition when scary, funny and downright bizarre scarecrows appear all around the village in gardens, on tractors and even under cars.

Children are welcome.

HOURS OPEN: 12 noon to 3pm and 7pm to 11pm, Tuesdays to Sundays. Closed Mondays.

BEERS: Farne Island Bitter and Tyneside Blonde from Hadrian and Border Brewery, plus John Smith's, Guinness, lagers, cider and a choice of 10 wines.

FOOD: served 12 noon to 2pm and 7pm to 9pm. Service from 6.30pm Saturdays and in the holiday season. Sunday lunch from 12 noon to 2pm (advance booking is advisable at weekends and in school holidays).

Sandwiches, baked potatoes, bar meals, a restaurant menu and a daily specials board. Specialities include fresh locally-caught seafood and river salmon in season, beef and lamb from local farms and pheasant from the local shoot. There is a choice of nine starters from £3.50, and main courses are between £7.95 and £17.95; Sunday roast £6.75, puddings £4.25.

HOW TO GET THERE: from the A1 at Alnwick, follow the B1340 via Denwick for three miles.

Mark and Louise Dean
The Horse Shoes Inn, Rennington Village,
Alnwick NE66 3RS.
Tel: (01665) 577665.
Email: mdean_678@msn.com

---

(26) *Stamford, near Rennington ~* **THE MASONS ARMS**

SINCE it first opened for business as a coaching inn 200 years ag
this family-run pub standing in a rural setting only a few mil
inland from Craster has grown in size by incorporating tw
adjoining cottages.

The traditional bar with dark beams and whitewashed wa
sparkles with a collection of old horse-brasses and there is a
interesting display of old photographs. A see-through old stor
fireplace with log-burning stove separates the bar from th
family room where paintings by local artists are displayed. Mea
are also served in an adjoining dining room. At the rear the
are two quiet gardens overlooking open fields. Children a
welcome.

HOURS OPEN: 12 noon to 2pm and 6.30pm to 11pm, Mondays to Saturdays; 12 noon to 2pm and 6.30pm to 10.30pm, Sundays.

BEERS: Bedlington Terrier from the Northumbrian Brewery, Gladiator Bitter and Secret Kingdom from Hadrian & Border Brewery, plus three guest cask ales; Theakstons, John Smith's, Worthington, Guinness, lagers, a choice of 18 wines and 20 malt whiskies.

FOOD: served 12 noon to 2pm, and 6pm to 9pm, daily.
Sandwiches, bar meals, and restaurant menu. Starters from £3.25 include crab salad and smoked fish soup, both £4.95. Main courses from £8.50 to £16.95 are locally sourced, including Northumbrian pork sausage and Northumbrian beef and lamb, also daily specials like venison and bramble casserole £8.95, and vegetarian dishes. Puddings £4.25, including Heckley High House sticky sponge.

ACCOMMODATION: 17 rooms, £75 to £95 per room.

HOW TO GET THERE: from Alnwick follow the B1340 coast road north for five miles.

**Robert Culverwell,
The Masons Arms, Stamford, near Rennington,
Alnwick NE66 3RX.
Tel: (01665) 577275.
Email: bookings@masonsarms.net**

NORTH

THE castles, fortified towers and battlefield sites in this area close to the Scottish border are reminders of a time when this was a violent frontier zone where rustling (reiving), plundering churches and blood feuds were commonplace and neither the laws of England or Scotland could be enforced.

On three of the main routes linking the two countries, pubs which began life as alehouses for sheep drovers or as 18th century coaching inns are found on the A68 at West Woodburn, on the A697 at Wooler and Milfield, and on the old A1 at Belford and Warenford.

Some are to be found in places a little off the beaten track including an ancient 17th century pub at Allerdean and an old coaching inn at Lowick, while others in villages attracting more visitors include the county's only thatched pub at Etal, and country pubs in Chatton and Eglingham.

Photograph:
Milfield Plain and the Cheviot Hills

(27) *Wooler* ~
THE ANCHOR INN

IN the market town known as the Gateway to the Cheviots, this recently refurbished 18th century inn is popular with walkers who need only walk a short distance to reach Wooler Moor and join

numerous way-marked footpaths — including the St Cuthbert's Way long- distance trail — into the high hills.

There is a tourist information centre at the top of the main street in Padgepool Place.

The well furnished bar and lounge is a real local with a well-used pool room, darts board, a display of sports trophies won by pub teams, Victorian photographs of farmworkers and townspeople and old posters about stolen sheep and horses. The cheerful landlady supervises the home-cooked meals which are served in the lounge and in a comfortable dining room. Old stone steps lead up to a small patio beer garden at the rear of the pub.

Children welcome.

HOURS OPEN; 6.30pm to midnight, Mondays; 12 noon to 4pm and 6.30pm to midnight, Tuesdays to Thursdays; 12 noon to 1am, Fridays; 11am to 1am, Saturdays; 11am to midnight, Sundays.

BEERS: Black Sheep, John Smith's, McEwans, Guinness and lagers.

FOOD: served 12 noon to 2pm and 6.30pm to 9pm, daily.

Sandwiches from £3.15, jacket potatoes and pub grub meals, £5.95 to £10.25, including home-made lasagne, steak and ale pie, minted lamb shanks, bangers and mash, and steaks. Sunday roast beef or roast pork lunches, £5.95; two courses, including home-made sticky toffee and pineapple upside down cake, £6.95. Children's menu.

ACCOMMODATION: one twin and one double en suite rooms, £50 double, £30 single B&B, plus a family room which sleeps four, £70.

HOW TO GET THERE: Wooler is 8 1/2 miles north of Powburn on the A697.

Carol Johnson,
The Anchor Inn, 2 Cheviot Street,
Wooler NE71 6LN.
Tel: (01668) 281412.
Email: the.anchor.inn@btconnect.com
www.anchorinnwooler.co.uk

(28) *West Woodburn ~* BAY HORSE INN

THIS late 18th century coaching inn stands next to an old stone bridge over the River Rede on a route once travelled by Roman soldiers, and which today is used by motorists following the A68 to Scotland.

There's a homely feel about the traditional, low-ceilinged bar which is probably open to serve customers' needs for more hours each day than any other pub in the county. As a village 'local' it has a corner with a pool table, darts board and TV, customers' tankards hanging above the bar counter and numerous hunting photographs taken here in the Border Hounds country.

From breakfast to supper time food is served either in the lounge bar or in an attractive 12-table restaurant, and outside in an enclosed beer garden next to stables where there is a children's play area.

HOURS OPEN: every day except Christmas Day, from 7.30am to midnight.

BEERS: Ruddles, John Smith's, Stones, Guinness and lagers.

FOOD: breakfasts or coffees with home-made cakes and biscuits served from 7.30am; lunches 12 noon to 2.30pm; evening meals 6.30pm to 9pm.

Sandwiches, finger nibbles, lasagne and chilli served all day. Home-cooked main courses (£7.95 to £14.95) using locally-sourced produce include mince and dumplings, Northumbrian sirloin steaks, roast local black-faced lamb, home-baked ham with Cumberland sauce, seafood and vegetarian options.Children's menu £3.95.

ACCOMMODATION: five en suite rooms, £42 double, £45 with four-poster bed.

HOW TO GET THERE: take the A68; it's four miles north of the minor road to Redesmouth and Bellingham and five miles south of the B6320 to Otterburn.

Mrs Hilda Wright,
Bay Horse Inn, West Woodburn, Hexham,
Northumberland, NE48 2RX.
Tel: (01434) 270218.
Email: enquiry@bayhorseinn.org

---

(29) *Etal ~*
THE BLACK BULL INN

THE county's only thatch-roofed pub, this 300 year-o
whitewashed building stands in the centre of the muc
photographed small village, just a short stroll from Etal Castle.

The long bar has an interesting clutter of memorabilia includin
an eye-catching collection of witch dolls around the bar serving are
and hanging from the low beamed ceiling. A very popular spot fo
drinks and bar meals in summer months: customers unable to fin
a table in the bar or in the restaurant can use tables outside the pu
and in the enclosed rear beer garden, where there is also a woode
smokers' shelter. Children welcome.

A miniature steam railway runs between the village and nearb
Heatherslaw Mill.

HOURS OPEN: 11am to 11pm weekdays in summer, 12 noon to 3pm and 6pm to 11pm in winter (closed Tuesday lunchtimes); 11am to midnight, Saturdays and 11am to 10.30pm, Sundays.

BEERS: Black Sheep, guest real ales, John Smith's and lagers.

FOOD: (except Tuesdays in winter) from 12 noon to 8.30pm Mondays to Thursdays, 12 noon to 9pm Fridays and Saturdays, 12 noon to 8pm Sundays.

Sandwiches from £3.25, bar meals and restaurant menu. Freshly cooked food using locally supplied ingredients. Main meals from £4 to £15 can include pan-fried trout with Pernod, steaks, smoked fish pie, steak and ale casserole, mince and dumplings, lasagne, home-made steak and ale and steak and black pudding pies; choice of eight vegetarian dishes. Desserts include locally-made Doddington ice cream.

HOW TO GET THERE: Etal is on the B6354, which runs from the A697 near Crookham to Berwick.

**Karen Hunter,
The Black Bull Inn, Etal,
Cornhill-on-Tweed TD12 4TL.
Tel: (01890) 820200.
Email: karenwichyp@aol.com**

---

(30) *Lowick ~*
Black Bull Inn

IN the original part of this attractive 18th century coaching inn the
is a traditional bar (which overlooks the village churchyard), a gam
room and a cosy snug bar. This leads into rooms added onto the o
inn where there is a 12-table restaurant and an adjoinin

conservatory dining room. There is a sheltered rear patio garden an
outdoor tables at the front of the pub.

Unusually, the inn has a coffee shop which provides mornin
coffees and afternoon teas. A focus for a variety of village activitie
and fundraising events, the Black Bull also holds monthly afternoo
tea dances.

Children welcome; dogs allowed in the front bar.

HOURS OPEN: 12 noon to 11pm or later, daily; coffee shop open 10am daily for breakfasts and coffees.

BEERS: Jennings, Theakstons, McEwans, John Smith's, lagers and a choice of 15 wines.

FOOD: served from 12 noon to 9pm, daily (advance booking advised for evenings).

Sandwiches using home-made bread £4.75. There is a lunchtime specials board for bar meals and a children's menu. The restaurant menu features local Glendale lamb and belted Galloway beef from Johnsons of Wooler, local fish from North Shields, Lindisfarne mussels and oysters, old English Heritage potatoes from Tiptoe Farm, Doddington ice creams and cheeses. Starters from £3.50 and main courses from £6.95 to £16.25.

ACCOMMODATION: three en suite rooms and one with private bathroom; B&B £35 single, double/twin £70. There is also a family room for three or more at £25 per person. The pub offers golfing accommodation packages and bikers have the use of a secure overnight garage.

HOW TO GET THERE: travel north up the A1 for five miles beyond Belford; turn left on to the B6353 at Fenwick.

**Dawn Scott,
Black Bull Inn, 2-4 Main Street, Lowick,
Berwick-upon-Tweed TD15 2UA.
Tel: (01289) 388228.
Email: John540Scott@btinternet.com**

(31) *Belford ~*
THE BLUE BELL HOTEL

THIS ivy-covered 18th century coaching inn, located midway between Alnwick and Berwick, can be found in the centre of this peaceful village which is now by-passed by the main road to Scotland. On a west-facing slope next to St Mary's parish church,

one of the most attractive features of this old hostelry is the large landscaped beer garden with its children's play area and views over open countryside to the west.

The traditional bar overlooks the Market Place; there is a bistro which serves bar meals and the Garden Restaurant which serves an à la carte menu and Sunday lunches.

Close to the Lindisfarne National Nature Reserve, Holy Island and the Farne Islands, Belford is on the route of the St Oswald's Way long-distance trail.

Children welcome.

HOURS OPEN: 11am to midnight, daily.

BEERS: Timothy Taylor, Black Sheep, Tetleys, Calders, Guinness, lagers, an extensive wine list and 12 malt whiskies.

FOOD: served 12 noon to 3pm and 6 to 9pm, daily.
Lunchtime triple-decker sandwich and snack menu. Bar meals, from £7.25, include beer battered Eyemouth cod or haddock, breaded whole-tail scampi, fish pie and a choice of eight salads. Children's menu from £4.75.
All menus use locally-sourced produce. À la carte starters, from £3.95, include steamed mussels in Lindisfarne mead. Seasonal main courses, from £12.80, range from local venison, Northumbrian lamb shank and freshly caught fish and seafood. Home-made desserts, a choice of local cheeses and a vegetarian menu.

ACCOMMODATION: 28 bedrooms, including two family rooms and two rooms for disabled guests; B&B from £45 per person.

HOW TO GET THERE: Belford lies 1/2 mile off the A1, 11 miles south of Berwick and five miles inland from Bamburgh.

Yvonne Douglas,
The Blue Bell Hotel, Market Place,
Belford NE70 7NE.
Tel: (01668) 213543.
Email: enquiries@bluebellhotel.com
www.bluebellhotel.com

---

(32) *Chatton* ~
THE PERCY ARMS HOTEL

BUILT as a hunting lodge by the Duke of Northumberland in 1839 the building became licensed 40 years later. Standing in the centre of this small village which lies only one mile from Chillingham Castle, this is the local pub for many families living in nearby farms

and dry hamlets. Walkers and cyclists are frequent visitors, along with holidaymakers heading inland from the nearby coast to escape a North Sea fret.

There is a good-sized, comfortable L-shaped bar which overlooks the front garden, plus a games room, a separate dining annexe and an oak-panelled restaurant which can seat up to 25 people. The attractive front garden has outdoor seating and tables on the lawn. Family-friendly; children welcome, but no dogs.

HOURS OPEN: 11am to 11pm, Mondays to Saturdays; 12 noon to 10.30pm, Sundays.

BEERS: Jennings' Cumberland Cream, Banks's Original, Marston's Pedigree and other guest cask ales, Guinness and lagers.

FOOD: served 12 noon to 2pm, and 6.30pm to 9pm, daily.
Sandwiches from £4.50. A daily specials board offers starters from £2.95 and main courses from £6.95 to £13.95 for a trio of Glendale lamb cutlets. Evening main course meals from £8.25 to £16.50 include home-made Craster kipper pate, Doddington chicken, Northumbrian beef and the famous Percy grill. There is an eight-choice children's menu and home-made puddings.

ACCOMMODATION: eight en suite rooms, B&B £80 double, £45 single.

HOW TO GET THERE: Chatton is on the B6348 between Wooler and the A1.

**Fiona and David Munro,
The Percy Arms Hotel, Main Road,
Chatton NE66 5PS.
Tel: (01668) 215244.
Email: percyarmshotel@gmx.com
www.percyarmshotel.co.uk**

(33) *Allerdean ~* **THE PLOUGH**

RIGHTLY proclaiming itself as an "ancient pub", this 17th century inn enjoys a quiet rural setting in open countryside only a few miles south-west of Berwick.

Its small rooms retain original features including stone walls, wood beam ceilings and open fires and there is an interesting collection of old farming implements. There is a traditional bar as well as three small intimate dining areas, and from the beer garden which has a children's play area there is an impressive panoramic view south into the Cheviot Hills.

Children are welcome up to 9pm.

HOURS OPEN: in summer, 12 noon to 3pm and 5pm to 11pm, daily; open all day in summer holidays. In winter, 6pm to 11pm, Tuesdays to Fridays; 12 noon to 2pm, Wednesdays (for a pensioners' special lunch); all day from 12 noon, Saturdays and Sundays; closed Mondays.

BEERS: two guest cask beers change weekly, which can include Black Sheep, Old Kiln Ale from the Border Brewery and Doom Bar from Cornwall; plus John Smith's, McEwan's, Guinness and lagers.

FOOD: served 12 noon to 2.30pm and 6pm to 9pm, daily.
Sandwiches, light lunches, daily bar meal and à la carte restaurant menus. Fresh fish and seafood from Eyemouth is a speciality, also beef and lamb supplied by nearby farms. Popular starters at £4.95 include fresh garlic mushrooms in cream cheese sauce and chef's home-made chicken liver pâté. Main courses from £7.95 to £17.95 include steamed local seafood platter in a cream cheese sauce, and fresh local sea bass and langoustine bake.

ACCOMMODATION: Caravan Club certificated location, electric hook-up £12 a night.

HOW TO GET THERE: Allerdean is five miles from Berwick: from the A1, follow the B6354 Duddo-Etal road or take the B6525 via Ancroft.

**Trevor McArdle and Jane Sylvester,
The Plough, Allerdean,
Berwick-upon-Tweed, TD15 2TD.
Tel: (01289) 387206.
Email: trevorgmca@aol.com
www.theploughinnallerdean.co.uk**

---

(34) *Milfield ~*
THE RED LION INN

ORIGINALLY a sheep drovers' inn that stood in open fields, the Red Lion — positioned midway between Newcastle and Edinburgh — was a busy coaching inn between 1785 and 1835, and the village of Milfield grew up around it. This listed building is a local pub for

those living in surrounding villages, and is popular with anglers and members of the nearby gliding club.

There is a small bar, an atmospheric lounge with a large, original stone fireplace, and a small dining room with four tables. Beyond the car park there is a beer garden overlooking fields, and the historic villages of Ford and Etal are only two miles to the north.

HOURS OPEN: 12 noon to 2pm and 6pm to 11pm, Mondays to Fridays; 12 noon to 11pm, Saturdays; 12 noon to 10.30pm, Sundays.

BEERS: guest cask beers change regularly — more than 130 have been offered in the past two years — plus Theakstons, John Smith's, Guinness, lagers and five house wines.

FOOD: served 12 noon to 2pm and 6pm to 9pm, Mondays to Fridays; 12 noon to 9pm, Saturdays; Sunday carvery lunches from 12 noon (advance booking advised at weekends).

All meals cooked by the chef/landlord feature locally-sourced produce. Speciality dishes on table menus include honey roast belly pork with bubble and squeak mash, sweet and sticky chicken and homemade steak and ale pie. Alternative dishes on a blackboard menu include six starters, light bites such as duck confit wraps in honey and soya sauce, £5.50 and main courses from £7.95 to £14.25, including lamb's liver and bacon, pan-fried salmon and three vegetarian dishes. Children's menu £3.95. Home-made puddings.

ACCOMMODATION: three en suite rooms, B&B £40 double, £25 single, including breakfast.

HOW TO GET THERE: Milfield is five miles north of Wooler on the A697.

Iain Burn,
The Red Lion Inn, Milfield NE71 6JD.
Tel: (01668) 216224.
Email: iaindburn@fsmail.net
www.redlioninn-milfield.co.uk

(35) *Eglingham* ~
THE TANKERVILLE ARMS

THIS imposing stone-built pub, dating from the 1830s, takes its name from the wealthy family which once owned half the village and much of the surrounding countryside. There is a smart,

comfortable bar with ceiling beams, an open fire and on the walls a variety of traditional sporting prints and old photographs.

The hub of this popular pub is its restaurant, which can seat up to 55 people, and a side room with four tables. This spacious and stylish dining area beneath exposed beams is adorned with old prints and a range of antiquated farm implements. There is a good sized, sheltered beer garden with a view over open countryside.

HOURS OPEN: on request from 10am for breakfast; 12 noon to 11pm, Mondays to Thursdays; 12 noon to 12.30am, Fridays and Saturdays; 12 noon to 10.30pm, Sundays.

BEERS: Black Sheep Bitter, Mordue's Workie Ticket and Born to be Mild, Tyneside Blonde from the Hadrian & Border Brewery, Boddingtons, Guinness, lagers and a choice of 33 wines.

FOOD: sandwiches from £4.95, served until 5pm; breakfast served until 2pm. Full menu available all day from 12 noon to 9.30pm (advance booking advised for the restaurant at weekends).

Two courses £17.95: popular main courses include Eyemouth hot smoked salmon and braised shoulder of Glendale lamb. Half portions for children / small appetites.

HOW TO GET THERE: from Alnwick follow the B6346 north-west for eight miles.

Claire and Derek Charlton,
The Tankerville Arms, 15 The Village,
Eglingham NE66 2TX.
Tel: (01665) 578444.
Email: charlton169@hotmail.com
www.tankervillearms.com

(36) *Warenford ~*
WHITE SWAN INN

ORIGINALLY an 18th century coaching inn when the main road t
Scotland passed through this small village, the stone-built pub nov
enjoys a tranquil location just off the modern A1 a few miles inlan
from Bamburgh.

There is a comfortable, spacious bar with beamed ceiling and
log fire in a large stone fireplace. Customers can sample free hom
made pickled eggs and shallots provided by one of the Swan'
regulars in return for a small donation to the Lucker village ha
fund.

The restaurant area — which has wheelchair access — has tw
distinctive dining areas, one decorated in contemporary style an

he second with whitewashed walls and a beamed ceiling. There is a secluded beer garden filled with the sounds of the pub's pet geese, ducks, turkeys and bantams.

Children welcome; dogs allowed in bar.

HOURS OPEN: 12 noon to 3pm and 5pm to closing time, daily.

BEERS: a selection of Wylam Brewery cask beers, plus John Smith's, Guinness, lagers and a choice of 30 wines and seven malt whiskies.

FOOD: served 12 noon to 2.30pm (3pm on Sundays) and 6pm to 9pm, daily.

Sandwiches, bar meals and a regularly changing restaurant menu which features local seafood and fish, and beef, lamb and pork supplied by named Northumberland farms.

Starters include home-made terrines, king scallops, mussels and fresh oysters from nearby Ross Sands. Main courses £8.95 to £16.50: specialities include whole lemon sole, roast cod, calves' liver and steak, Guinness and oyster pie. Home-made puddings include brulées and chocolate and almond truffle cake.

A children's menu offers a choice of five meals at £5.

HOW TO GET THERE: Warenford is just off the A1 three miles south of Belford, and 4 1/2 miles inland from Bamburgh.

**Andrew and Diane Hay,
White Swan Inn, Warenford,
Belford NE70 7HY.
Tel: (01668) 213453.
Email: dianecuthbert@yahoo.com**

SOUTH WEST

THIS corner of Northumberland, once famous for its lead mines and now for its wildlife-rich high heather moorland, lies within the North Pennines Area of Outstanding Natural Beauty.

Two of the favourite pubs in this section, found along the scenic route which takes motorists into Cumbria and the Lake District, are located near Langley and in the West Allen village of Whitfield.

In the East Allen valley, which has an attractive mixture of deciduous woodland, upland sheep farms and grouse moors, there are pubs with character in Allendale — once the 'capital' of the lead mining district, and at Allenheads which is the most southerly and highest pub in this book. The fifth favourite is located further to the east in gentle walking country close to the village of Slaley.

Photograph:
The River Allen

95

(37) *Allenheads ~*
THE ALLENHEADS INN

LOCATED in the centre of this small North Pennine community, which at 1,500 feet above sea level is one of the highest villages in England, the 200-year-old inn is a welcome stop for walkers and

cyclists, particularly those reaching this high midway point on the long-distance Coast to Coast cycle route. It has a comfortable bar with a log fire and bookshelves, a snug and a games room.

There is an interesting collection of stuffed birds and animal heads in the restaurant and tables outside the pub overlook the village square where there are several Victorian red-painted lead mining carts. At the nearby Allenheads Heritage Trust Centre visitors can see the village as it would have looked in the lead mining boom days of the 1840s and follow a nature trail.

Children welcome; dog-friendly.

HOURS OPEN: 12 noon to midnight, Mondays to Saturdays; 12 noon to 11.30pm, Sundays.

BEERS: Black Sheep, Greene King Abbot, Boddingtons and guest real ales.

FOOD: served 12 noon to 2pm and 7pm to 9pm, daily.
Sandwiches, bar meals and a restaurant menu. Starters from £3.99; main courses from £7.50 include vegetarian dishes, Cumberland sausages, steak pie, curries and lamb shank. Sunday lunches feature locally-reared beef, lamb and pork.

ACCOMMODATION: seven rooms, all en suite, B&B single £31, double £54.

HOW TO GET THERE: from Allendale Town, follow the B6295 south for eight miles.

Ann and Philip Homer,
The Allenheads Inn, Allenheads,
Hexham NE47 9HJ.
Tel: (01434) 685200.
Email: philann@phomer.fsbusiness.co.uk

---

(38) Langley ~
THE CARTS BOG INN

STANDING on a road leading to the Lake District described as one of the 10 most scenic drives in Europe, this ivy-covered inn was opened in 1775 when a local entrepreneur began selling ale to the drivers of coal carts who became stuck in nearby boggy ground.

Despite its isolated location the pub has a dedicated core of regulars from nearby farms and villages, and the young owner has deliberately preserved its old-fashioned, traditional character. There are log fires and displays of old photographs and Victorian prints depicting life in this lead mining area of the North Pennines.

The restaurant extends into the original inn's stone cow byre where there is a hayloft collection of old metal advertising signs, beer jugs, bottles and locally hand-made Langley bricks. The one-acre beer garden has picnic tables, two quoits pitches, a decked wooden shelter for smokers, and overlooks open fields and moorland.

Children welcome; well-behaved dogs allowed in the bar.

HOURS OPEN: 12 noon to 2.30pm, Tuesdays to Fridays; 5pm to 11pm, Mondays to Fridays; 12 noon to 11pm, Saturdays; 12 noon to 10.30pm, Sundays.

BEERS: Allendale Brewery Best Bitter, Mordue's Carts Bog Best Bitter, John Smith's, Guinness and lagers. Real ales change weekly.

FOOD: served 12 noon to 2pm, Tuesdays to Sundays; 6.30pm to 9pm, daily (advance booking advised).

A speciality is locally-sourced produce and seasonal game. The lunchtime blackboard menu, which changes almost every day, offers a choice of 8 starters from £4, and up to 11 main courses all under £9. These include liver and bacon, and haddock cooked in a light crispy batter made from real ale with hand-cut chips.

HOW TO GET THERE: from Haydon Bridge, follow the A686 towards Alston for three miles.

Kelly Norman,
The Carts Bog Inn, Langley on Tyne,
Hexham NE47 5NW.
Tel: (01434) 684338.
www.cartsbog.co.uk

---

(39) *Whitfield ~*
THE ELK'S HEAD

THIS traditional, family-owned pub in the wooded West Allen valley stands on the scenic road through south-west Northumberland which continues through Alston to the Lake District.

It's an unpretentious riverside pub which serves as the local for farmers, shepherds and gamekeepers, as well as a refreshment stop for walkers coming off the surrounding North Pennine moors, and there is often a collection of wellies and muddy boots left in the entrance porch.

To one side of the bar is a small dining area with coal fire, and a games room. There is also a small restaurant which has a number of photographs of prize-winning bulls and terriers. The small beer garden was recently extended and now stretches down to the banks of the River Allen next to the old stone Blue Back Bridge, on a stretch of the river which is popular with canoeists and anglers.

HOURS OPEN: 12 noon to 11pm, daily in summer; closed some afternoons in winter.

BEERS: Golden Plover from Allendale Brewery, John Smith's, McEwans, Guinness, lagers and cider.

FOOD: 12 noon to 2.30pm, daily; 6.30pm to 9pm, Tuesdays to Sundays.
Sandwiches from £2.65. Home-cooked bar meals: starters from £2.95 include black pudding topped with poached egg (£3.95) and mussels (£4.75). Main courses (£5.45 to £8.95) include pizzas, pastas, various pies, mince and dumplings, and steaks. Take-away fish and chips on Friday nights, £4.75.
Children's menu.

ACCOMMODATION: nine en suite bedrooms, double B&B from £50.

HOW TO GET THERE: the pub is on the A686, 12 miles from Hexham and nine miles from Alston.

Darren Scott and Lorna Prentice,
The Elk's Head, Whitfield, Hexham NE47 8HD.
Tel: (01434) 345282.
Email: elkshead@btconnect.com
www.elksheadwhitfield.com

(40) *Allendale ~*
THE GOLDEN LION

CENTRALLY positioned in the Market Place – where the village's famous New Year's Eve burning tar barrel ceremony takes place – this 17th century, three-storey building has a comfortable bar with a log fire that usually has a dog lying in front of it. There is a side

dining room and a games room displaying photographs of the tar barrel ceremony.

The explanation for the pub's intriguing wolf theme (there's a Wolf Bitter and a wolf and beef pie on the menu) is that the last wild wolf in England was shot nearby 300 years ago, while in 1904 armed farmers roamed the countryside after a wolf escaped from a travelling menagerie and began attacking sheep in the area.

Sunday lunches are served in an upstairs dining room. The pub is used on many evenings for local community meetings, including the Dale Singers, Allendale Lions and the local drama group. A traditional music night is held on the last Wednesday of every month.

HOURS OPEN: 12 noon to 12 midnight, Sundays to Thursdays; 12 noon to 1am Fridays and Saturdays.

BEERS: Allendale Brewery's Wolf, Black Grouse and Best Bitters, Nel's Best (High House Farm), Wylam Gold Tankard, Black Sheep; plus Caffreys, John Smith's, Guinness and lagers, and a choice of 20 malt whiskies.

FOOD: served 12.30pm to 2pm and 6pm to 9pm, daily.
Sandwiches, baked potatoes and a blackboard daily menu offering chicken, ham and leek pie, steak and ale pie, fish pie, gammon and Northumbrian lamb and steaks. Starters from £3.25, main courses from £6.45 to £9.50.

HOW TO GET THERE: Allendale Town is on the B6295, seven miles south of Hexham.

Gloria and Ian Armstrong,
The Golden Lion, Market Place,
Allendale NE47 9BD.
Tel: (01434) 683225.
Email: Gloria.hollybush@talk21.com

(41) *Slaley ~*
THE TRAVELLER'S REST

THE history of this roadside inn, which enjoys an attractive rural setting one mile outside Slaley village, dates back to the 16th century when it was built as a farmhouse. Established as an inn in the 1840s, many original features have been preserved.

The flagstone floor and clusters of wooden bench seats forming seating areas around open fires create a pleasant, old-fashioned atmosphere in the bar area and there is a cosy six-table restaurant with a low beamed ceiling. A sign on a chair carved straight from a tree trunk warns the superstitious that several local women have become pregnant after sitting on it.

There is a large lawned beer garden with a view over open fields and a children's adventure play area. Nearby attractions include Slaley Hall golf course and the Derwent Reservoir.

Children welcome and dog-friendly.

HOURS OPEN: 12 noon to 11pm, daily.

BEERS: Allendale Best Bitter, Wylam Gold Tankard, Black Sheep, John Smith's, Guinness and lagers.

FOOD: served 12 noon to 3pm, daily and 5pm to 9pm, Tuesdays to Saturdays.
Sandwiches from £4.75. All-day traveller's breakfast available. Popular dishes on the lunchtime menu include salmon and prawn crêpe with a fish cream sauce, and a classic club sandwich with chicken and bacon.
Starters from £4.25, main courses from £9 to £15.
The à la carte evening menu offers a choice of seven starters including pan-fried sea bass, and specialities among 11 main courses include duck with honey and ginger sauce, venison with apple and blackberry reduction, and cod with scallops and scampi.

ACCOMMODATION: three en suite bedrooms, B&B £60 double.

HOW TO GET THERE: follow the B6306 south from Hexham for four miles; the pub is one mile north of Slaley village.

**Jed Irving,
The Traveller's Rest, Slaley,
Hexham NE46 1TT.
Tel: (01434) 673231.
Email: info@1travellersrest.com**

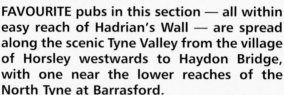

TYNEDALE

FAVOURITE pubs in this section — all within easy reach of Hadrian's Wall — are spread along the scenic Tyne Valley from the village of Horsley westwards to Haydon Bridge, with one near the lower reaches of the North Tyne at Barrasford.

The capital of Tynedale, Hexham, grew around an impressive 12th century abbey which occupies the site of a Saxon church built by St Wilfrid 500 years earlier. In a wooded valley at Dipton Mill, just two miles south of this ancient market town, is probably the smallest pub in the county.

Favourites close to the banks of the Tyne are found in the historic village of Corbridge, in Haydon Bridge and at Warden, close to the junction of the North and South Tyne rivers. Three pubs on the north side of the Tyne which all offer fine views over the valley are found at the hillside hamlet of Anick, and in Fourstones and Horsley. Across the Tyne, several miles to the south another favourite, is the 200-year-old village pub at Hedley on the Hill.

Photograph:
Hexham Abbey

(42) *Barrasford ~* *BARRASFORD ARMS*

GIVEN that owner-chef Tony Binks worked with Albert Roux, it's not surprising that this Victorian country pub is renowned for its food. Still serving as the local in this quiet village, the bar which overlooks the beer garden has dark wood settles, a log fire and a cosy, friendly feel.

In the two dining rooms, which can seat up to 60 people, signature dishes developed jointly by Roux and Tony Binks are shown in framed displays. There is also a small private dining room for private lunch and dinner parties.

Tables in the patio area and beer garden enjoy views across to Haughton Castle on the far bank of the North Tyne. There's also a children's play area and a small wooden smokers' den in the front garden.

HOURS OPEN: 6pm to 12pm, Mondays; 12 noon to 2.30pm and 6pm to12pm, Tuesdays to Fridays; 12 noon to 11pm, Saturdays and Sundays.

BEERS; guest cask ales include Nel's Best, Gladiator and Wylam Gold Tankard; plus John Smith's, McEwan's, lagers and a choice of eight wines.

FOOD: served 12 noon to 2pm, Tuesdays to Saturdays, 12 noon to 3pm, Sundays; evening meals 6.30 to 9pm, Mondays to Saturdays (advance booking advisable).

Menu and specials board change daily offering traditional English cooking with French influences, using high-quality Northumbrian beef and lamb and other seasonal, locally-sourced food. A three-course lunch (£14.50) offers a choice of four starters, main courses and desserts. The evening menu offers starters from £4.50 and main courses from £9.50. Specialities include a twice-baked cheese soufflé starter, braised rump of beef in brown ale and seared wild sea trout.

ACCOMMODATION: seven en suite rooms, B&B single £65, double £85. Also camping barns which sleep up to 16 people.

HOW TO GET THERE: from Chollerford on the B6318 (Military Road) follow the A6079 north, then take the minor road from Chollerton. Barrasford is seven miles from Hexham.

Tony Binks,
Barrasford Arms, Barrasford, Hexham NE48 4AA.
Tel: (01434) 681237.
Email: contact@barrasfordarms.co.uk
www.barrasfordarms.co.uk

---

(43) *Corbridge ~*
THE BLACK BULL

AN attractive old building in the heart of this historic Tynedale village, the Black Bull dates back to 1766 and there has been a pub here since the mid-19th century.

The main recently refurbished L-shaped bar retains its original stone floors, low beams and fireplaces. At one end of the bar there is a snug area and at the other a 12-table restaurant with windows looking out onto the street. A second restaurant area with exposed stone walls and a beamed ceiling has nine tables.

There is wheelchair access but nearby parking space in the Market Square is at a premium, particularly in summer months, so be prepared for a short walk.

Only a few yards from the pub is the Anglo-Saxon church of St Andrew and a 14th century fortified Vicar's Pele tower.

HOURS OPEN: 11am to 11pm, daily.

BEERS: Old Speckled Hen, Ruddles, Greene King IPA, plus guest real ale, Guinness and lagers.

FOOD: available from 12 noon (last orders 9pm), Mondays to Saturdays; 12 noon to 8pm, Sundays. Advance booking advised at weekends.

Sandwiches and jacket potatoes £3.95 to £5.25. Lunch menu light bites (£4.95 to £8.95) include a house deli board and a smoked fish platter. Specials from £8.45 to £10.45 include roast duck, steak and kidney pudding and slow-cooked beef ribs. Evening restaurant main courses (£6.85 to £10.95) include fish of the day, seafood, chicken and chorizo paella, and a vegetarian risotto. Children's menu until 7pm.

HOW TO GET THERE: several roads lead off the A69 Newcastle to Hexham road into Corbridge.

David and Lynda Wears,
The Black Bull, Middle Street,
Corbridge NE45 5AT.
Tel: (01434) 632261.
Email: 7639@greeneking.co.uk

(44) *Warden* ~
THE BOATSIDE INN

A RIVERSIDE pub, The Boatside was built in the early 1800s and before the sturdy Warden bridge was built customers had to cross the South Tyne at this point by ferry.

Meals are served in the bar and lounge which have an informal, comfortable atmosphere, and by cheerful waitresses in the main restaurant and conservatory which overlook the riverside. Food and drinks can also be taken outside on a sheltered patio and in the beer garden. There is a large car park and a wooden shelter for smokers.

The North and South Tyne rivers converge at the Meeting of the Waters, a short walk from this old inn. Nearby Warden parish church, which dates from the 11th century and was built with stones taken from Chesters Roman fort, has the oldest Saxon tower in the county.

Children welcome.

HOURS OPEN: 11am to 11pm, Mondays to Saturdays; 12 noon to 11pm, Sundays.

BEERS: a choice of guest cask ales including High House Auld Hemp, Mordue's Workie Ticket and Black Sheep, plus John Smith's, Boddingtons, Guinness and lagers.

FOOD: served 12 noon to 2pm and 6.30pm to 9pm, Mondays to Fridays; 12 noon to 2.30pm and 6.30pm to 9pm, Saturdays; 12 noon to 9pm, Sundays.

Sandwiches, bar meals, restaurant menu using locally-sourced produce. Main courses (£7.95 to £14.50) include home-made dumplings with mince, steak and Guinness pie, home-made curries, smoked salmon with prawn salad. Sunday roasts with a choice of Aberdeen Angus beef, pork, lamb and chicken, £8.50.

ACCOMMODATION: three en suite rooms, B&B £70 per room; also self-catering cottages.

HOW TO GET THERE: from Hexham follow the A69 for 2 1/2 miles west, then turn right for Warden, 1 mile.

The Boatside Inn, Warden, Hexham NE46 4SQ.
Tel: (01434) 602233.
Email: sales@theboatsideinn.com
www.theboatsideinn.com

(45) *Dipton Mill ~*
DIPTON MILL INN

BUILT on the site of an old farmhouse and mill which burned down in the 1780s, this small country pub was opened as an ale house in 1822 to serve passing sheep drovers.

The inn's Boston creeper-covered frontage featured in an episode of TV series The Likely Lads. It is probably the smallest pub in the county and it serves a choice of real ales made by the landlord in his own micro-brewery.

Entry to the pub is through a low doorway into the traditional bar which has a stone floor, dark wood-panelled walls, log fires, a low beamed ceiling and a collection of horse brasses and old pewter tankards. There are only 10 tables, so 40 people can (and frequently do) fill the room to enjoy Janet Brooker's tasty home cooking. When weather permits, meals are also served at tables in the pub's small, sheltered garden next to the Dipton Burn.

HOURS OPEN: 12 noon to 2.30pm and 6pm to 11pm, Mondays to Saturdays; 12 noon to 3pm, Sundays.

BEERS: Devil's Elbow, Shire Bitter, Devil's Water, Whapweasel and Old Humbug, all from the Hexhamshire Brewery, plus a choice of 18 wines and 22 malt whiskies.

FOOD: lunches served between 12 noon and 2.30pm; evening meals from 6.30pm to 8.30pm.

A selection of sandwiches and salads and a choice of bar meals from a blackboard menu. Starters from £2.50. Main courses, from £5.50 to £8, may include Northumbrian cheese ploughman's lunch, braised steak, duck breast, home-cooked steak and kidney pie, and bacon chops in cider sauce. Home-made puddings include Eyemouth tart, and apple and blackberry crumble.

HOW TO GET THERE: Dipton Mill lies two miles south of Hexham on the B6306 to Whitley Chapel; it is 1 1/4 miles from Hexham Racecourse.

**Geoff Brooker,
Dipton Mill Inn, Dipton Mill Road,
Hexham NE46 1YA.
Tel: (01434) 606577.
Email: ghb@hexhamshire.co.uk**

(46) *Hedley on the Hill ~ THE FEATHERS INN*

THIS 200 year-old stone-built pub high above the Tyne valley was once frequented by lead miners and cattle drovers. Today customers travel considerable distances to reach the quiet, hilltop village and

enjoy the inn's old-fashioned atmosphere and high-quality food prepared by the joint owner/chef, who has worked in three kitchens each awarded one Michelin star.

Both bar areas have an old-fashioned, homely feel with open fires, tankards hanging from exposed beams, and jars filled with cough candy and sarsaparilla tablets. There are two quiet side rooms for diners and a few outdoor tables in front of the pub. Children welcome.

Special events at the Feathers include farmers' markets, wine nights, whisky tasting evenings and an Easter beer and food festival.

HOURS OPEN: 12 noon to 11pm, Tuesdays to Saturdays; 12 noon to 10.30pm, Sundays; 6pm to 11pm, Mondays.

BEERS: a choice of four guest real ales, including brews from the nearby Wylam Brewery; a large range of malt whiskies, an extensive wine list and old-fashioned dandelion and burdock, elderflower wine and wild nettle cordial.

FOOD: served 12 noon to 3pm, weekends; 6pm to 9pm, Tuesdays to Sundays (advance booking advised).

Snacks, sandwiches, bar meals and a restaurant menu, featuring regional British food with a classical French influence; the menu of locally-sourced seasonal food changes daily. Lunch starters and light snacks (£3 to £6) include a home-made charcuterie board, and celeriac coleslaw toast and pickles; main courses (£7 to £11) can include surprises such as jugged grey squirrel. The evening menu usually offers a choice of six or more starters and six main courses from £9; popular dishes include home-made black pudding, hot smoked eel, a 19th century-style pheasant curry, slow-cooked mutton, oysters and venison pie.

HOW TO GET THERE: from the A695 at Stocksfield, take the New Ridley road south, keep left and climb up to Hedley on the Hill.

Rhian Cradock and Helen Greer,
The Feathers Inn, Hedley on the Hill,
Stocksfield NE43 7SW.
Tel: (01661) 843607.
Email: info@thefeathers.net
www.thefeathers.net

---

(47) *Haydon Bridge ~ GENERAL HAVELOCK INN*

THERE'S more to this family-run village pub than meets the eye. Behind its black-painted frontage there's a comfortable bar with an open fire and piano and this leads through into a restaurant —

formerly a stone barn — with a high beamed ceiling, chandeliers, military memorabilia and a river view. At the rear of the pub there is a patio area with a marquee for outdoor eating in summer months and a private garden which borders the River South Tyne.

The building dates back to 1788 and is named after a military hero born in 1795 some miles away in County Durham who died from dysentery in India in 1857. The general became a household name when he led troops in the successful relief of Lucknow during the Indian Mutiny. His mother lived at nearby Bardon Mill.

There is some on-street parking and this main road will become considerably quieter when the A69 Haydon Bridge by-pass opens in 2009.

HOURS OPEN: 12 noon to 2.30pm and 7pm to 10.30pm, Tuesdays to Sundays; closed Mondays.

BEERS: High House Nel's Best, Derwentwater Bitter, Mordue's Five Bridge Bitter, Wylam Bitter, John Smith's, Guinness, lagers and a choice of 35 wines.

FOOD: served 12 noon to 2pm and 7pm to 9pm, Tuesdays to Saturdays; 12 noon to 2pm, Sundays.

Sandwiches, bar meals and restaurant menu; advance booking is advised at weekends. Favourite starters include cheese croquettes and potato cake with black pudding and red onion marmalade. Chef's specials, from £7.95, include beef, Guinness and wild mushroom stew, fresh mussels in season, fillets of plaice steamed in a light puff pastry case, pasta and vegetarian dishes. Home-made desserts or cheeseboard, £4.75.

HOW TO GET THERE: follow the A69 west from Hexham for 4 1/2 miles; Haydon Bridge is four miles from the Roman Wall.

Gary and Joanna Thompson,
General Havelock Inn, Radcliffe Road,
Haydon Bridge NE47 6ER.
Tel: (01434) 684376.
Email: generalhavelock@aol.com

(48) *Horsley ~* *LION AND LAMB*

THE oldest part of this whitewashed village pub was originally built as a farmhouse in 1718, and became a coaching inn a quarter of a century later when the main highway between Newcastle and Carlisle ran through the village.

The main L-shaped bar has great character with a flagstone floor and a low beamed ceiling. A low doorway leads into a high-ceilinged barn-style room with exposed stone walls, alcoves and a loft level containing an array of farm implements. There are leather settees and armchairs and one large wooden refectory table which seats up to 16 people.

The rustic-style restaurant has exposed old timbers and ceiling beams, with poems and famous quotations about Northumberland adorning the walls. This room leads onto a large terrace which offers good views over the Tyne valley and is used as an outdoor dining area in summer months. There is a large beer garden and a children's adventure play area.

HOURS OPEN: 12 noon to 11pm, Mondays to Saturdays; 12 noon to 10.30pm, Sundays.

———————————————

BEERS: Auld Hemp from High House Brewery, Flowers IPA, Boddingtons, Bass, Guinness and lagers.

———————————————

FOOD: served 12 noon to 2.30pm and 6pm to 9.30pm, Mondays to Saturdays; 12 noon to 3pm and 7pm to 9pm, Sundays.
Tapas snacks from £2.50 to £5.95, hot sandwiches £5.95. Lunch menu choices include tagliatelle and crab and seafood salad. Two-course lunch meal deal £8.95, children's menu £2.95 to £3.95. Evening meals offer starters from £3.95 to £4.95, followed by a good selection of poultry, fish and meat dishes, including beef and Boddingtons pie, sizzling hot plates and steaks, costing from £7.95 to £12.95.

———————————————

HOW TO GET THERE: the village is signposted off the A69, two miles west of Heddon-on-the-Wall.

———————————————

Anthony Milne,
Lion and Lamb, Horsley,
Newcastle upon Tyne NE15 0NS.
Tel: (01661) 852952.
Email: tonymilne6@hotmail.com

———————————————

(49) *Anick* ~
THE RAT INN

AN old drovers' inn built around 1750, this ivy-covered pub is tucked away up a narrow lane on the edge of a hillside hamlet only one mile from Hexham.

The young owners have purposely maintained its traditional character, particularly in the bar, which has a counter made from an antique oak sideboard and chamber pots hanging from the ceiling. There is an equally atmospheric lounge bar with logs burning in a cast-iron range. Tables in the dining room and small conservatory look out onto sheltered terraces and a colourful garden filled with shrubs, flower tubs and hanging baskets which has a fine view over the Tyne valley.

No-one knows for sure how the pub acquired its odd name, but regulars are happy to offer visitors their own favourite theories.

Children welcome; dogs allowed only in the garden.

HOURS OPEN: 12 noon to 3pm, 6pm to 11pm, Mondays to Fridays; 12 noon to 11pm, Saturdays; 12 noon to 10.30pm, Sundays.

BEERS: a choice of locally-brewed cask ales, plus Eucharis IPA, John Smith's, Bass, Guinness, lagers, and a wine list including eight wines sold by the glass.

FOOD: served 12 noon to 2pm and 6pm to 9pm, Tuesdays to Saturdays; 12 noon to 3pm, Sundays (advance booking advised at weekends). Only sandwiches on Mondays.

The lunchtime bar menu offers sandwiches (£3.95) and light snacks such as home-made Scotch eggs. A specials board, which changes daily, offers a choice of eight main courses from £8.95 to £28.50 (for roast Northumbrian rib of beef for two). Favourites include braised beef in Allendale Bitter and slow-roast shoulder of lamb. A board in the bar indicates which local farm has supplied the day's beef, lamb and pork.

HOW TO GET THERE: across the river bridge north of Hexham, at the A69 roundabout, take the sign-posted minor road to Anick.

**Phil Mason and Karen Erdington,
The Rat Inn, Anick, Hexham NE46 4LN.
Tel: (01434) 602814.
Email: info@theratinn.com
www.theratinn.com**

---

(50) *Fourstones ~*
THE RAILWAY INN

ORIGINALLY a small village pub built 150 years ago close to the old village station, the Railway has been imaginatively extended to create a restaurant which overlooks the beer garden and enjoys fine views over the Tyne valley.

There are two comfortable bar areas: one has displays of old railway photographs and steam train drawings and the other has a collection of victorious Newcastle United team photographs from the early 1900s. The restaurant comprises a ground level, wooden-floored dining area which seats 20 and overlooks the shrub-filled pub garden, and an upper dining area can accommodate a further 30 people.

Children welcome; dogs allowed in garden.

HOURS OPEN: 5pm to11pm, Mondays; 12 noon to 3pm and 5pm to11pm, Tuesdays to Thursdays; 12 noon to 11pm, Fridays to Sundays.

BEERS: Jennings and Marstons real ales, plus guest local cask beers, Guinness and lagers.

FOOD: served 5pm to 9.30pm, Mondays; 12 noon to 2.30pm and 5pm to 9.30pm, Tuesdays to Thursdays; 12 noon to 9.30pm, Fridays and Saturdays; 12 noon to 5pm, Sundays.

Sandwiches £4.50, daily specials from £5.50, bar meals and restaurant menu featuring locally-sourced meat, venison in season and locally-caught salmon. Starters from £3.50, main courses from £6.50 to £14.95. Popular specialities are Derwentwater duck oven-baked with hedgerow fruits, Balmoral fillet steak on a bed of haggis, Fourstones fowl, chicken supreme filled with locally-cured pancetta and shallots, and the chef's fresh home-made pies which include braised rabbit, beef and drunken mushroom, and pork with whole-grain mustard and redcurrants.

Children's menu: choice of seven main courses from £2.95.

HOW TO GET THERE: Fourstones lies on the B6319, three miles from Haydon Bridge and two miles from the B6318 Military Road at Chesters Roman Fort.

David and Lynn Meldrum,
The Railway Inn, Fourstones, Hexham NE47 5DG.
Tel: (01434) 674711.
Email: the.railway.inn@hotmail.co.uk

MICRO-BREWERIES

MANY of the pubs listed in this book give you the chance to sample beers brewed by some of the following micro-breweries.

ALLENDALE BREWERY

Allendale Brewing Company, Allendale, Hexham NE47 9EQ.
Tel: (01434) 618686

The brewery is the dream of father-and-son Jim and Tom Hick, who brewed their first batch on Valentine's Day 2006.

Beers include: Allendale Best Bitter (3.8 per cent); Curlew's Return (4.2); Golden Plover (4.0) and Allendale Wolf (5.5).

HADRIAN & BORDER BREWERY

Unit 10, Hawick Crescent Industrial Estate, Newcastle NE6 1AS.
Tel: (0191) 2765302

Created when Border brewery, formed in 1992, moved from Berwick and took over the premises of Four Rivers brewery, formerly the Hadrian Brewery.

The plant produces ten different real ales including: Vallum Bitter (3.6 per cent); Gladiator Bitter (4.0); Farne Island Pale Ale (4.0); and Tyneside Blonde (3.9).

HEXHAMSHIRE BREWERY

Leafields, Ordley, Hexham NE46 1SX. Tel: (01434) 606577

The brewery was set up in 1992 in a redundant farm building by the owner of the Dipton Mill Inn, Geoff Brooker, and two partners. It is still brewing following the break-up of the owning partnership.

Beers include: Devil's Elbow (3.6 per cent); Shire Bitter (3.7); Devil's Water (4.1); Whapweasel (4.8) and Old Humbug (5.5).

HIGH HOUSE FARM BREWERY

Matfen, Newcastle NE20 0RG. Tel: (01661) 886192

The brewery was founded in 2003 by fourth generation farmer, Steven Urwin, who decided to diversify after the foot and mouth outbreak in 2001. All the beers are named after animals on the farm.

The brewery produces three permanent beers: Auld Hemp, (3.8 per cent), Nel's Best (4.2) and Matfen Magic (4.8) and several seasonal beers.

WYLAM BREWERY

South Houghton, Heddon-on-the-Wall, NE15 0EZ. Tel: 01661 853377

Wylam Brewery was set up in an old farm dairy near Heddon-on-the-Wall by Robin Leighton and John Boyle and the first brew was casked in 2000. Sadly Robin died in April 2005 but his three daughters have retained his interest.

Beers include: Wylam Bitter (3.8 per cent); Gold Tankard (4.0); Magic (4.2) and Silver Ghost (5.0).

READER REPORT
OR RECOMMENDATION

We would be delighted to receive readers' reports either about pubs included in this book or other pubs they feel should be considered for inclusion in the next edition of *Favourite Northumbrian Pubs*.

PUB ....

ADDRESS ....

....

MY NAME ....

CONTACT DETAILS ....

....

(This information will not be given to a third party)

COMMENTS

....

....

....

....

*(Comments accepted only on this printed form –
no photocopies please)*